EYEWITNESS ◉ ART

COLOR

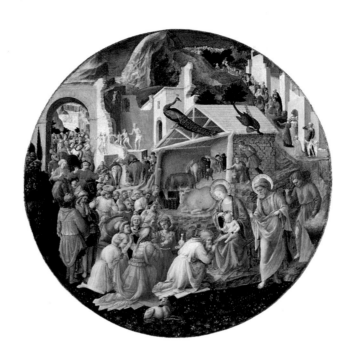

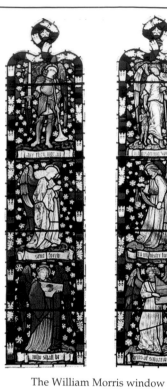
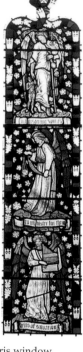

The William Morris window

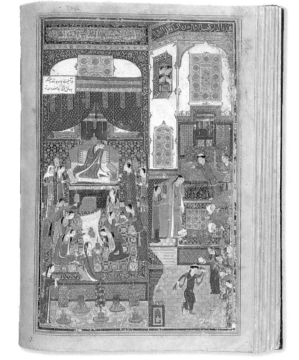

Moroccan rose and green tunic

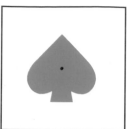

The "afterimage" illusion

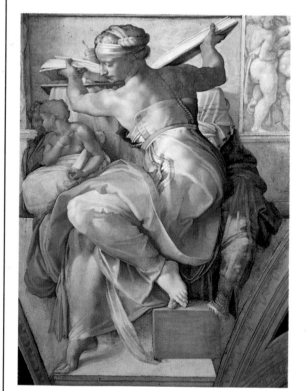

Persian manuscript illumination

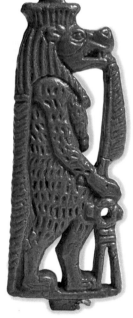

Egyptian blue-glazed
ceramic of a god

Michelangelo, *Libyan Sibyl*, c.1508;
after restoration

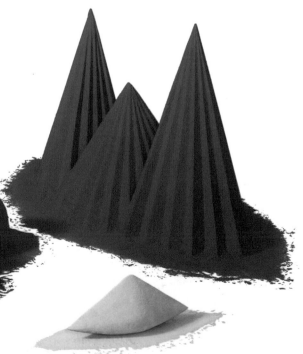

Anish Kapoor, *As if to Celebrate I Discovered a
Mountain Blooming with Red Flowers*, 1981

EYEWITNESS ART

COLOR

ALISON COLE

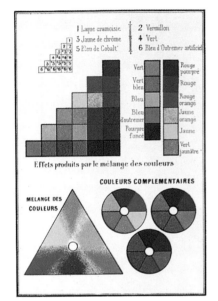

Frontispiece to Ogden Rood's
"Colors and Applications"

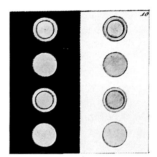

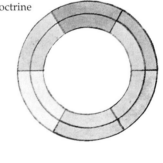

Details from
Goethe's "Doctrine
of Colors"

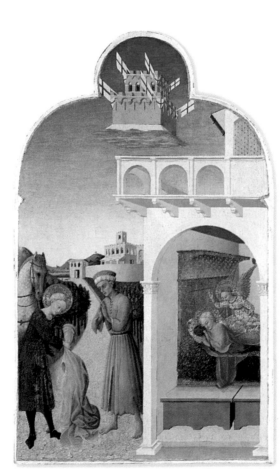

Sassetta, *The Wish of the Young St. Francis
to Become a Soldier*, 1437/44

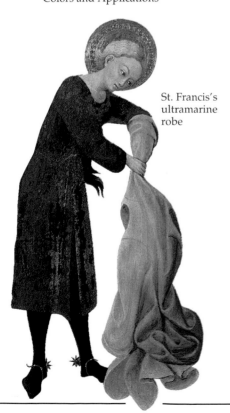

St. Francis's
ultramarine
robe

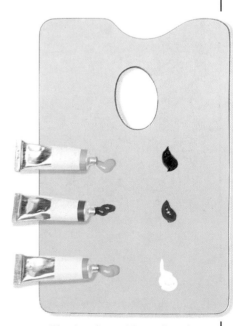

Plastic palette with acrylic paints

DK

DORLING KINDERSLEY

LONDON • NEW YORK • STUTTGART

IN ASSOCIATION WITH
THE NATIONAL GALLERY OF ART,
WASHINGTON, DC

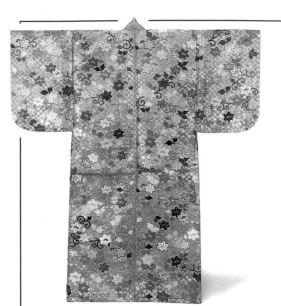

Japanese Noh costume

Azurite

Lapis lazuli

Vermilion

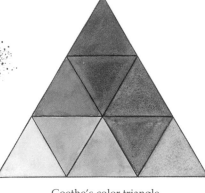

Goethe's color triangle

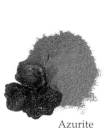

A DORLING KINDERSLEY BOOK

Editor Luisa Caruso
Designer Claire Pegrum
Assistant editor Louise Candlish
Design assistant Simon Murrell
Senior editor Gwen Edmonds
Managing editor Sean Moore
Managing art editor Toni Kay
U.S. editor Laaren Brown
Picture researchers Julia Harris-Voss, Jo Evans
DTP designer Zirrinia Austin
Production controller Meryl Silbert

For the National Gallery of Art, Washington, DC
Technical Consultants: Barbara H. Berrie, Conservation Scientist;
E. Melanie Gifford, Research Conservator for Painting Technology

First American edition, 1993
2 4 6 8 10 9 7 5 3 1

First published in the United States by
Dorling Kindersley, Inc., 232 Madison Avenue
New York, New York 10016

Library of Congress Cataloging-in-Publication Data

Cole, Alison.
    Color / by Alison Cole. -- 1st ed.
       p.   cm. -- (Eyewitness art)
    Includes index.
    ISBN 1-56458-332-5
    1. Color in art. 2. Color--Psychological aspects. I. Title.
II. Series.
ND1490.C66 1993   93-8066
752--dc20   CIP

Color reproduction by GRB Editrice s.r.l.
Printed in Italy by A. Mondadori Editore, Verona

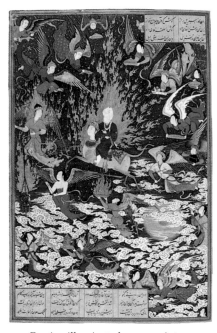

Persian illuminated manuscript

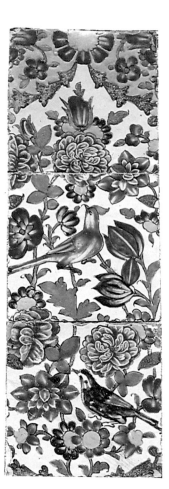

Persian tiles with bird
and flower designs

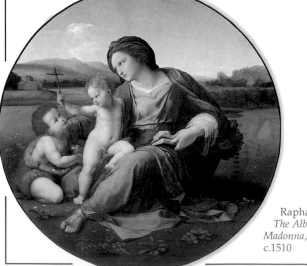

Egyptian coarse
paintbrushes

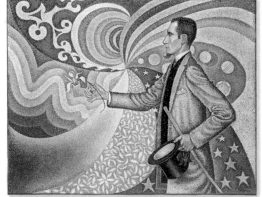

Raphael,
*The Alba
Madonna,*
c.1510

Paul Signac,
*Portrait of
Félix Fénéon
in 1890,*1890

Contents

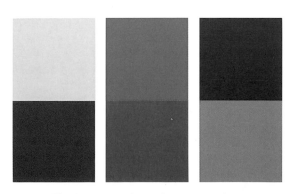

The three pairs of complementary colors

What is color?

THERE ARE NO "REAL" COLORS IN NATURE – only the various wavelengths that make up light, which are absorbed and reflected by all the objects around us. The reflected wavelengths enter the eye, which, in turn, sends signals to the brain: only then do we "see" the miracle of color. The sensation of white is created by the simultaneous impact of all these wavelengths on the eye. This white light contains the colors of the rainbow, which can be seen when the rays are separated by a glass prism. Each color has its own wavelength: violet has the shortest and red the longest. When these colors are combined with nature's pigments – the chlorophyll in grass, for instance – millions of shades can be created. Painters reproduce these using the powdered colors of natural or artificial pigments (p. 62) – which are themselves only the color of the light they reflect.

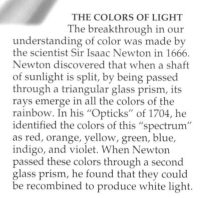

THE COLORS OF LIGHT
The breakthrough in our understanding of color was made by the scientist Sir Isaac Newton in 1666. Newton discovered that when a shaft of sunlight is split, by being passed through a triangular glass prism, its rays emerge in all the colors of the rainbow. In his "Opticks" of 1704, he identified the colors of this "spectrum" as red, orange, yellow, green, blue, indigo, and violet. When Newton passed these colors through a second glass prism, he found that they could be recombined to produce white light.

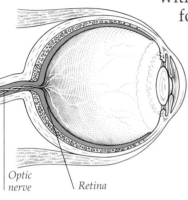

Optic nerve   *Retina*

THE WORKINGS OF THE EYE
Light enters the eye and hits the retina, where it is absorbed by rod and cone cells (so called because of their shapes). These cells transmit the signals that light triggers via the optic nerve, directly to the visual center at the back of the brain: color is truly "in the mind of the beholder." The three types of cones are sensitive to red, blue, and green wavelengths, and seem to be responsible for color vision in daylight. In dim light, the rods take over; they are more sensitive to blue-green light and distinguish clearly between values of light and shade.

Painted colors, however bright, are always duller than the colors of light

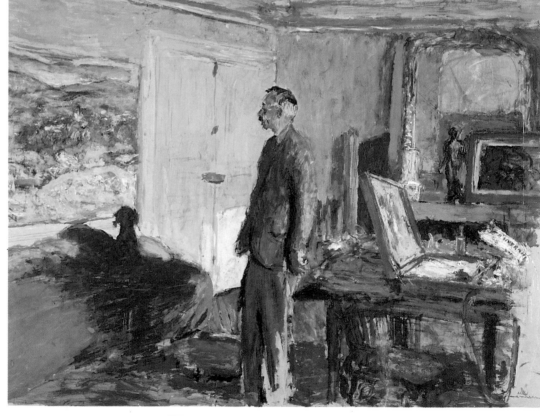

STUDY FOR A PORTRAIT OF BONNARD
Edouard Vuillard; c.1930; 45 x 56¼ in
(114 x 143 cm); distemper on paper, mounted on canvas
This study by the Post-Impressionist artist Edouard Vuillard (1868–1940) suggests the enchantment that color holds for the painter. Vuillard has painted a fellow artist, Pierre Bonnard (pp. 48–49), standing in his studio, inspecting a brightly colored landscape that he has just completed. The open paintbox (detail, left) represents not only the surface on which Bonnard has laid out his paints, but also his "palette" – the range of colors used. These consist of pigment (powdered color) suspended in a liquid known as a "medium" (p. 62), which gives the colors their paintlike consistency.

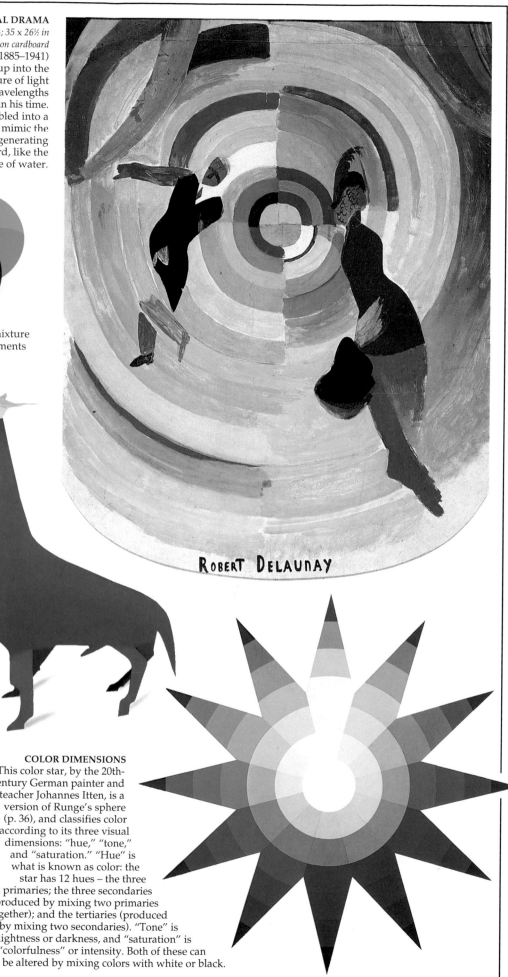

POLITICAL DRAMA
Robert Delaunay; 1914; 35 x 26½ in
(88.7 x 67.3 cm); oil and collage on cardboard
The 20th-century French painter Robert Delaunay (1885–1941) was intrigued by the way light could be broken up into the colors of the spectrum, and by the dynamic nature of light waves. These behave just like the electromagnetic wavelengths used by radio, which was a thrilling new invention in his time.

Here, the rainbow is pulled apart and reassembled into a brilliant pattern of revolving arcs and rings. These mimic the impact of waves of light as they strike the eye, generating the same vibrating energy. Colors radiate outward, like the ripples created by a pebble as it hits the surface of water.

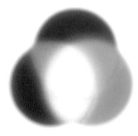

"Additive" mixture of primary lights

"Subtractive" mixture of primary pigments

PRIMARY LIGHTS AND PRIMARY PIGMENTS
A century after Newton's "Opticks," it was discovered that white could be produced by mixing just three parts of the spectrum: red (orange-red), green, and blue (blue-violet) (above left). These primary lights can be "added" together to produce all possible color sensations (red and green make yellow) and are also those to which the eye is most sensitive. However, when the three purest primary colors in pigment – used in modern color printing and known as cyan (greenish-blue), yellow, and magenta (bluish-red) – are mixed, they produce black (above right). This is because pigment strongly "subtracts" or absorbs light, so that it only reflects the color of the remaining wavelengths.

HORSE
Alexander Calder; 1970; height:
38½ in (97.5 cm); cut, bent, and
painted sheet metal; both sides
For centuries, the colors red, blue, and yellow have been identified as the "primaries" of the painter. They cannot be created by mixing colors, and artists like Alexander Calder (1898–1976) delighted in their bright simplicity. These differ subtly from the purer printers' primaries described above, which are produced by mixing two primaries of light (above left).

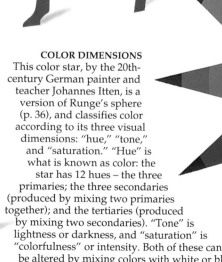

COLOR DIMENSIONS
This color star, by the 20th-century German painter and teacher Johannes Itten, is a version of Runge's sphere (p. 36), and classifies color according to its three visual dimensions: "hue," "tone," and "saturation." "Hue" is what is known as color: the star has 12 hues – the three primaries; the three secondaries (produced by mixing two primaries together); and the tertiaries (produced by mixing two secondaries). "Tone" is lightness or darkness, and "saturation" is "colorfulness" or intensity. Both of these can be altered by mixing colors with white or black.

Ancient materials

THE COLORS OF PREHISTORIC, Egyptian, and Roman painting reflect the rituals and symbols of their diverse cultures, as well as the limited range of materials that were available. The earliest pigments were made from naturally occurring colored earths – white chalk, the reds, browns, and yellows from ochres, and darker umbers – and black charred wood. Dyes from animals and plants were soon exploited (although these colors often faded in light), as were the lasting, brilliant colors of minerals. To prepare paint, particles of pigment were ground into a "medium" – a binding agent like wax, egg, or tree resin – that made them workable and bound them to the paint surface. Synthetic colors, created through chemical processes, had also been developed by early Egyptian times.

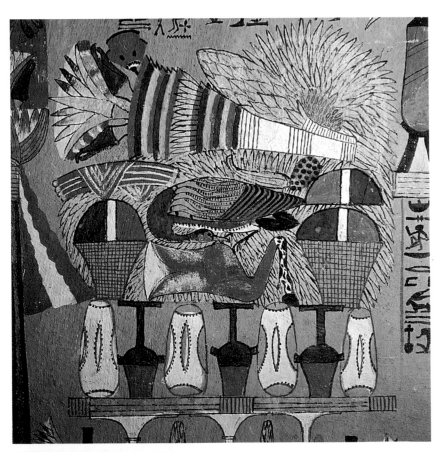

PREHISTORIC COLORS
The cave paintings at Lascaux in southwest France, dating from c.12000 B.C. (above), reveal the earliest colors used by mankind. The main pigments, red ochre and black, symbolic of life (blood) and death, were usually created from red earth colored by iron oxides and burnt charcoal or bone. They were mixed with animal fats, then warmed to make them workable. Yellow ochre was also used, while the sparkling white of the calcite crystals that lined the walls of the cave was skillfully incorporated into the overall scheme.

FOOD FOR A BANQUET
This Egyptian painting of the 19th Dynasty (c.1320–1200 B.C.), from the Tomb of Sennedjem, uses the typical Egyptian colors of white, black, turquoise, red, ultramarine blue (shipped from Afghanistan), and yellow ochre. The colors still appear so fresh and vibrant because they are mostly made from natural mineral substances, which do not tend to alter or fade. The dead, for whom the tomb painters laid on this rich banquet, were later to feature in the creation of a color of their own: "mummy brown," used for a time in the 17th and 18th centuries, was made from ground-up embalmed bodies!

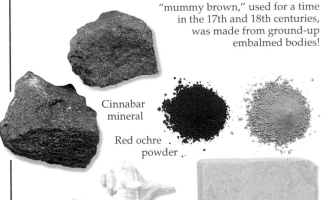

Cinnabar mineral

Red ochre powder

Whelks, from which Tyrian purple was made

Block of yellow ochre, and ground powder

Charcoal

Malachite mineral

ANCIENT PIGMENTS
These are some of the principal colors used by ancient civilizations. Stone Age man painted with charcoal, red ochre, and yellow ochre (the block above is freshly dug from the earth). The Egyptians ground the mineral malachite to make green (their color for the Nile), while the Romans used a new bright red – discovered by the ancient Chinese – made from cinnabar. They also prided themselves on Tyrian purple, a dye extracted from shellfish at Tyre in the Mediterranean, which came to symbolize wealth and imperial power.

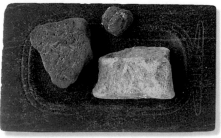

Basalt palette and paint grinder, with "frits"

EGYPTIAN EQUIPMENT
This palette and grinder were found in Thebes, along with coarse paintbrushes (right). They are shown with colored "frits" (mixtures of chemicals used in glass manufacture), which were ground and mixed with gum, probably from the acacia tree. Another synthetic pigment was Egyptian blue (top right), a compound of silica, copper, and calcium. It is likely that this was borrowed from the glassy blue glazes that coated ceramics (far right).

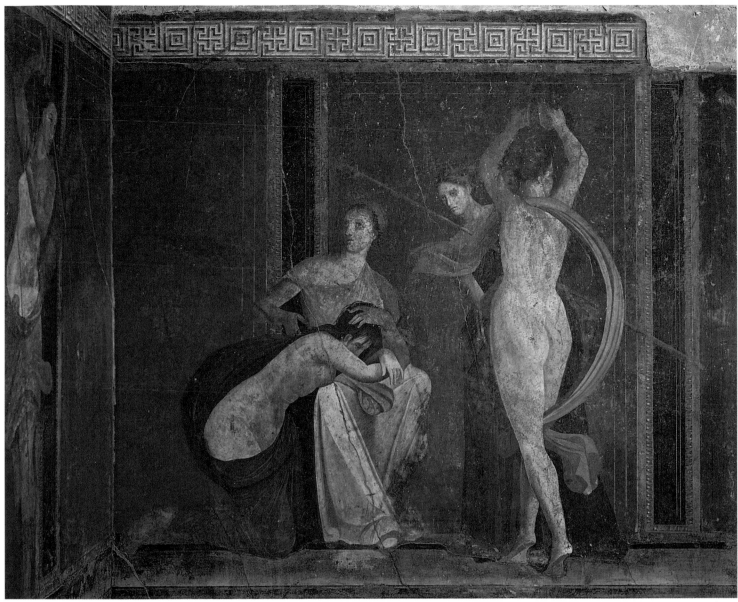

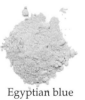

Egyptian blue

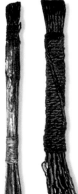

Palm fiber and
twig brushes, c.1450 B.C.

Blue-glazed
ceramic of
a god

Flagellation Scene

The Hall of the Mysteries, Pompeii; c.60 B.C.; fresco

The dramatic red that enlivens the wall panels of the
Hall of the Mysteries is vermilion, made from cinnabar,
which was used for the most sumptuous decorations. It
was mined in Spain and was so expensive to buy that a
law was passed setting a ceiling price. Apart from its
prohibitive cost, cinnabar also posed technical problems,
turning black on exposure to light. It had to be covered
with a protective coat of wax and oil, which was then
heated and polished with linen cloths and waxed cords.

ROMANO-EGYPTIAN FUNERARY PORTRAIT

2nd century A.D.; encaustic wax on panel

This striking portrait was painted for the exterior of a coffin. Originally
the head of the deceased would have been immortalized in stone, but
painting was cheaper and could be remarkably lifelike. Here, the
sculptural character has been preserved through
the encaustic wax technique, in which burnt-in
wax colors are handled with a fine knife to give
a sense of depth and texture. The secret of this
method was lost, although some have tried to
reinvent it: it seems that beeswax was melted
with an alkali, mixed with resin, and colors
were ground into it using a warm stone.

Beeswax

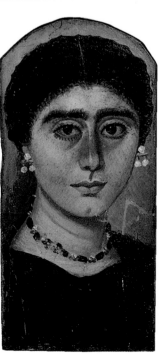

The splendor of gold

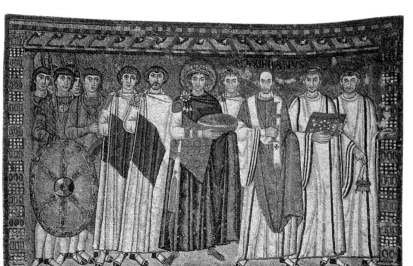

GOLD, THE MOST PRECIOUS METAL OF ALL, has been used by artists and craftsmen around the world to symbolize the glory of the heavens. Its color – whether warmed by an underlayer of red clay or tinged with green from natural impurities – gave an otherworldly quality to the sacred image, which seemed to rest on a bed of solid gold. In the Byzantine and medieval eras, the splendor of gold mosaic or gleaming burnished leaf represented two different levels of reality: the mystical realm of the heavenly sphere, and a pictorial world, created through suggestions of light and shade. When gold was illuminated by candles, the effect was dazzling, inspiring religious wonder and awe.

ALTAR VESSELS
Jewel-encrusted altar vessels – like this French chalice of the Abbot Suger of St. Denis (c.1140) – were designed to impress with their luster and opulence. The precious gems and gleaming metals multiplied the reflected light.

MOSAIC CUBES
This detail from the mosaic shows how the individual faces of the tesserae were set irregularly in the plaster to reflect the light unevenly, creating a shifting, sparkling surface of rich color.

THE COURT OF JUSTINIAN
The art of mosaic flourished under the rule of Constantinople (Byzantium), in the so called Byzantine era (476 A.D. onward). As distinct from Greek and Roman mosaics, made up of tesserae (Latin: "cubes") of marble set in plaster, Byzantine mosaics were created from colored glass. This allowed for a richer range of color, including the use of gold. In this mosaic (c.574 A.D.) from San Vitale in Ravenna, Italy, gold unites the Empress Theodora and the court with the glory of God.

THE ASCENSION OF MOHAMMED
In this Persian manuscript (1539–43), gold is used to invoke the spiritual splendor of the Prophet Mohammed's ascension to Paradise. The flaming haloes behind the Angel Gabriel and Mohammed burn brightly in the blue nocturnal darkness. The Prophet's face is left blank – he is too holy to be shown – and his dress is sober and unadorned. The red, green, yellow, and blue of the angels' garments combine to create an ecstatic play of color across the page.

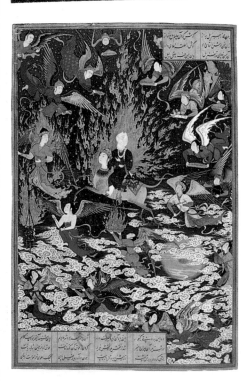

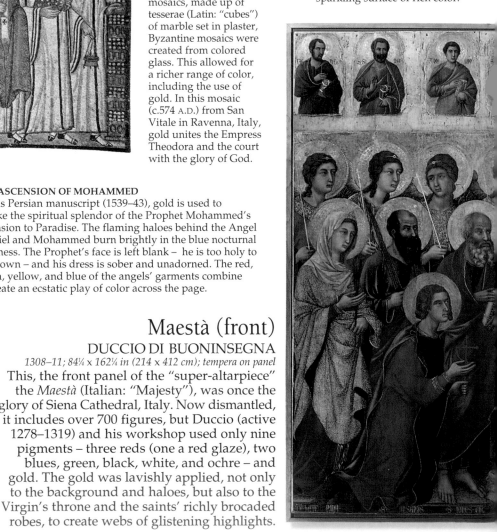

Maestà (front)
DUCCIO DI BUONINSEGNA
1308–11; 84¼ x 162¼ in (214 x 412 cm); tempera on panel
This, the front panel of the "super-altarpiece" the *Maestà* (Italian: "Majesty"), was once the glory of Siena Cathedral, Italy. Now dismantled, it includes over 700 figures, but Duccio (active 1278–1319) and his workshop used only nine pigments – three reds (one a red glaze), two blues, green, black, white, and ochre – and gold. The gold was lavishly applied, not only to the background and haloes, but also to the Virgin's throne and the saints' richly brocaded robes, to create webs of glistening highlights.

ELABORATE BROCADE

This detail from the *Maestà* shows how precisely Duccio rendered the fabric of St. Catherine's cloak: fine white lines and gold twirls are painted over a greenish gray base, and red is touched into the crosses. Each white line is meticulously edged with red, to make it stand out from the green.

TEXTILE PATTERNS

This 14th-century Sicilian silk textile, inspired by Oriental examples, reflects the Italian taste for intricacy of pattern and texture. Gorgeous fabrics, whether worn by the high clergy or the court, were considered to be a reflection of heavenly glory and the riches of God's creation.

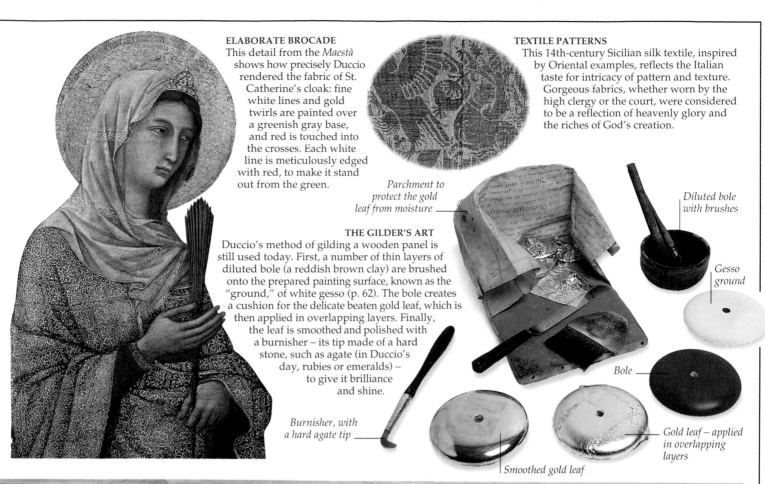

Parchment to protect the gold leaf from moisture

THE GILDER'S ART

Duccio's method of gilding a wooden panel is still used today. First, a number of thin layers of diluted bole (a reddish brown clay) are brushed onto the prepared painting surface, known as the "ground," of white gesso (p. 62). The bole creates a cushion for the delicate beaten gold leaf, which is then applied in overlapping layers. Finally, the leaf is smoothed and polished with a burnisher – its tip made of a hard stone, such as agate (in Duccio's day, rubies or emeralds) – to give it brilliance and shine.

Diluted bole with brushes

Gesso ground

Bole

Gold leaf – applied in overlapping layers

Burnisher, with a hard agate tip

Smoothed gold leaf

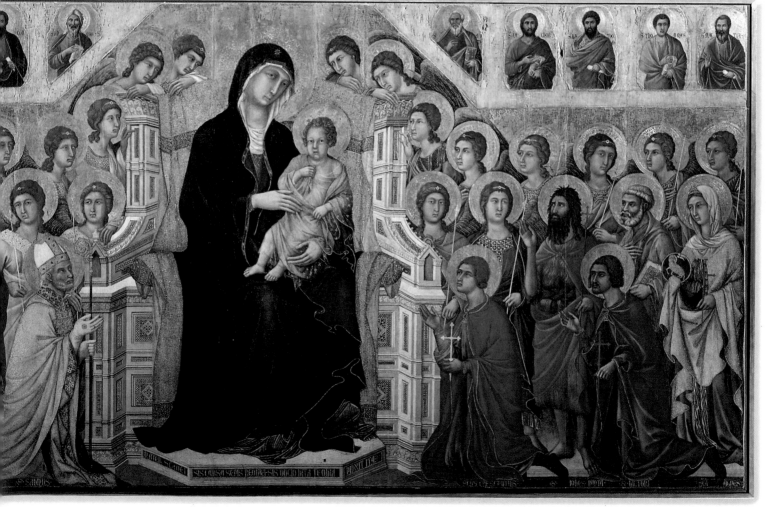

Fresco technique

THE ANCIENT ART OF TRUE FRESCO (Italian: *buon fresco*) was revived by the great Florentine masters Giotto (c.1267–1337) and Masaccio (1401–28). In this method of wall painting, powdered pigments are mixed with water and laid on a ground of damp plaster, which is made up of lime plus sand or marble dust. As the lime dries and the water evaporates, a hard crystalline surface is formed in which the color is bound. This means that the colors have to be applied rapidly; otherwise, the hues can darken (Michelangelo even grumbled about his colors becoming "moldy"). Many colors must be avoided altogether, because they react chemically with the lime or water: vermilion and lead white, for instance, oxidize and turn black. Others, like azurite blue, must be applied *a secco* – that is, on dry plaster. As the fresco dries, all of the hues lighten – and this also has to be taken into account.

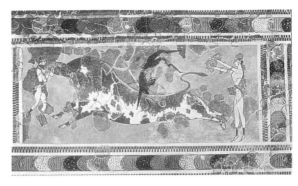

THE TOREADOR FRESCO
The Minoans – whose civilization ran parallel with that of the ancient Egyptians (c.2300–1100 B.C.) – seem to have been the first to use the true fresco technique. This mural from the Palace of Knossos in Crete, painted in about 1500 B.C., reveals a harmonious natural palette of pale yellow ochres and red iron oxides. These are mingled with other mineral pigments that evoke the colors of the Mediterranean sea.

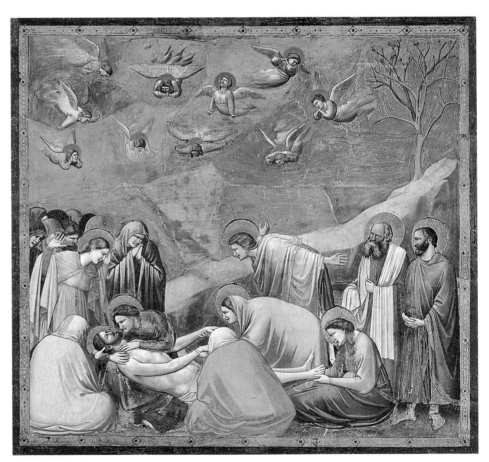

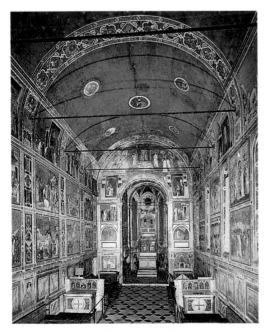

THE ARENA CHAPEL
Giotto's famous fresco cycle of "The Lives of the Virgin and Christ" in the Arena Chapel in Padua, Italy, makes extensive use of the mineral pigment azurite. This beautiful blue colors the skies and runs like a thread through the entire narrative. It echoes the symbolic blue of the chapel vault, which represents the heavens. Unfortunately, azurite has to be applied *a secco*, which has made the blue particularly vulnerable: some patches have fallen away, while others have greened due to the reaction of the pigment with high levels of carbon dioxide.

LAMENTATION OVER THE DEAD CHRIST
Giotto; c.1306; 78¾ x 72¾ in (200 x 185 cm); fresco
Giotto's innovative fresco technique relied on the "dish system." Colors were mixed in separate dishes to his precise specifications: pure powdered color, blended with water, would be prepared for the shadows, the same color with white for the mid-tones, and the color mixed with still more white for the lights. The accuracy of the dish system was very important, for the fresco was worked in daily sections of fresh, damp plaster, and colors had to be matched from one batch to the next. The hairline joins (detail, right) show these *giornate* sections (from the Italian: *giorno*, meaning "day"). Apart from the sky, they tend to outline separate color areas, which is why the figures are mostly clothed in robes of one hue.

FRESCO LAYERS

True fresco is built up in layers on a dry wall. A mortar of coarse sand, lime, and water is applied on top, followed by a coarse plaster of three parts sand and one part lime. Then comes the *arriccio*, another rough plaster, on which the fresco design (the "sinopia," executed in sinoper, a red earth) is drawn. The smooth final layer, the *intonaco*, is only ⅛ in (3–5 mm) thick and is made up of sand or marble dust, and fine lime in equal quantities.

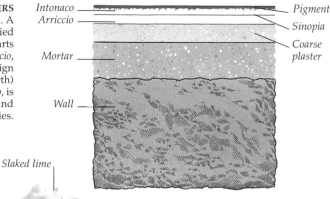

Intonaco — *Pigment*
Arriccio — *Sinopia*
— *Coarse plaster*
Mortar
Wall

Sinoper (red earth)   Raw umber

Raw sienna   Green earth

Chalk   *Bianco di San Giovanni*   *Slaked lime*

CREATING FRESCO WHITES

Because lead white turns black in fresco, slaked lime (burnt lime combined with water) provides the finest fresco white, although chalk is also recommended in early manuals. Giotto used the paste known as *Bianco di San Giovanni*, a dried, ground lime treated with vinegar.

FRESCO COLORS

Since pigments derived from plants were sensitive to the alkali in the lime, fresco colors were fairly limited; earth colors were its staples (above).

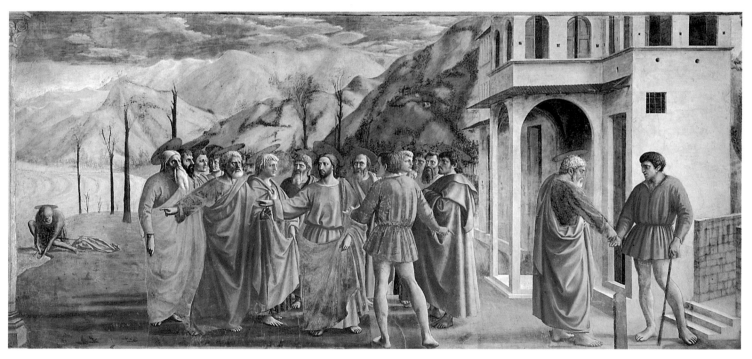

THE TRIBUTE MONEY

Masaccio; c.1425; 88½ x 235½ in (225 x 598 cm); fresco
Masaccio's recently restored fresco shows a palette of rich earth colors – roses, browns, oranges, and greens – combined with blue mixtures, lime white, and carbon black. He has chosen ordinary colors in the interests of naturalism and harmony; the colored robes flow into one another (their hems seem to elide) or are subtly contrasted: blue, for instance, against green. There are no outlines to interrupt the suggestion of light and space, and no brilliant colors (p. 62) applied *a secco*.

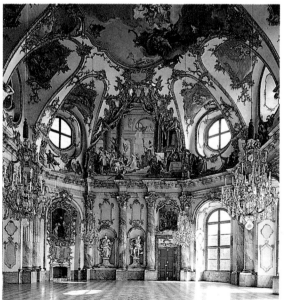

TIEPOLO'S DECORATIVE COLORING

The radiant frescoes painted in the 18th century by the Venetian painter Giambattista Tiepolo (1696–1770) still feature a surprisingly small range of colors. In his frescoes for the Würzburg Palace in Germany (left), painted in 1751, a wealth of sunny colors complements the superb architecture of white, gold, and patterned marble. Many of these are inspired mixtures: the warm oranges are Tiepolo's own blends of simple red and yellow pigments.

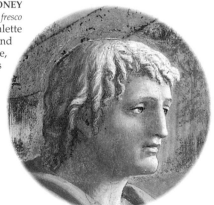

ST. JOHN

Masaccio has given his apostles tanned complexions so that the "white" light falling on the skin is more sharply defined. In this detail, the undermodeling (p. 62) in green shows through the flesh, especially in the areas of shadow.

The value of color

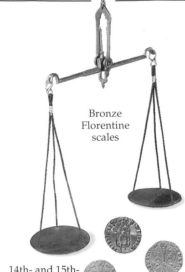

Bronze Florentine scales

14th- and 15th-century florins

IN EARLY ITALIAN PAINTING, color symbolism was an eminently practical affair. While some theorists tried to associate the different colors with the planets or the four elements of nature – red for fire, blue for air, green for water, and gray for earth – the artist was led by more pragmatic concerns. The most important factors, for the artist and the patron who commissioned him, were the quality and cost of the colors. Ultramarine blue, the jewel of them all, was extracted from the lapis lazuli stone, after it had been quarried and shipped from Afghanistan – its name, *oltremarine*, means "from across the seas." Because of its costliness, ultramarine was used for the most significant figures in the artist's narrative, the finest grades being reserved for Christ and the Virgin. The only colors that equaled ultramarine in intensity were vermilion, used for other key players, and pure gold.

PREPARING ULTRAMARINE
After being crushed in a mortar, lapis lazuli was incorporated into a mixture of viscous materials, such as oils and honey, wrapped in a cloth, and kneaded with an alkali – all to extract its violet-blue.

Lapis lazuli

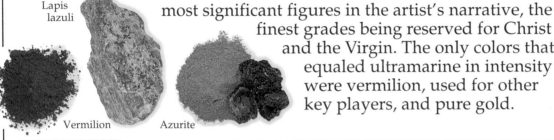

Vermilion

Azurite

WEIGHING IMPORTANCE
Colors were sold by weight. The finest grades of ultramarine, distinguishable by their deep violet undertone, were sold at two to four florins an ounce. Blue at four florins to the ounce might be stipulated for the Virgin, while one florin to the ounce would do for the rest.

THE BRIGHTEST RED
An artificial vermilion was developed from sulfur and mercury, and became one of the most reliable pigments. It was bought by the lump, and then ground, to make sure that it had not been secretly mixed with red lead or brick.

THE CORONATION OF THE VIRGIN
Enguerrand Quarton; c.1453–54; 72 x 86½ in (183 x 220 cm); tempera on panel
Many contracts drawn up between the patron and painter specified the use of only the best-quality pigments. The detailed contract for this altarpiece states that the main blues must be ultramarine, although cheaper "German" blue, azurite (above), could be used for the frame. The finest ultramarine adorns the robe of the Virgin, which is echoed in the deep blue sky below. The use of blue, gold, and vermilion relates to the different levels of Christian devotion: gold and red were associated with the worship of the Trinity, saints, and angels; and blue with the Virgin.

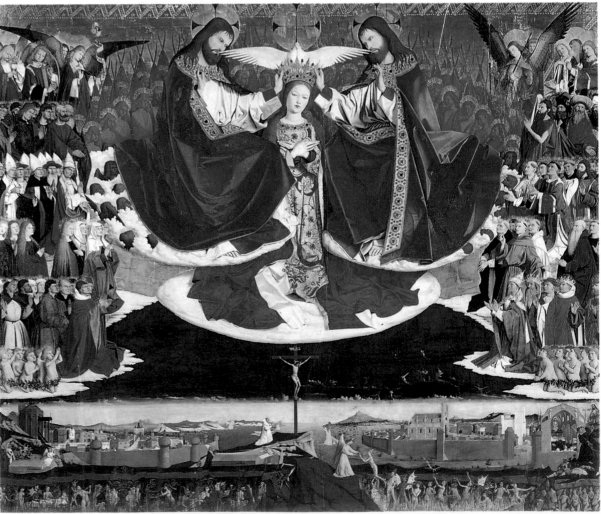

Color symbolism

During the early Renaissance period (14th and 15th centuries), colors were considered to exist in a symbolic hierarchy. Their importance was dictated both by value and by the "divine" status accorded to pure, brilliant hues. This was a continuation of the medieval idea that bright, clear colors are a reflection of the beauty of God's creation, while mixed colors are "corrupted." Aside from this, color was used according to the fashionable tastes and the storytelling conventions of the time. Saints, for instance, were often identified by the colors of their robes, while other meanings could be understood from the way that color was used in context.

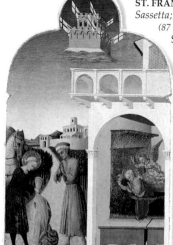

THE WISH OF THE YOUNG ST. FRANCIS TO BECOME A SOLDIER
Sassetta; 1437/44; 34¼ x 20¾ in (87 x 52.4 cm); tempera on panel
St. Francis's charity is emphasized by the fineness of the robe he is giving away – in pure ultramarine. This color is echoed in the star-spangled canopy above his bed of gold, where he dreams of the religious order he is to found (this episode of the story appears in the same panel). The combination of blue and gold was often identified with Christianity.

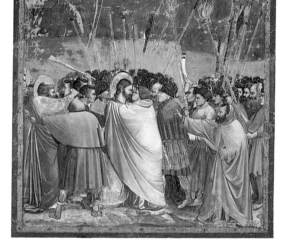

Yellow ochre

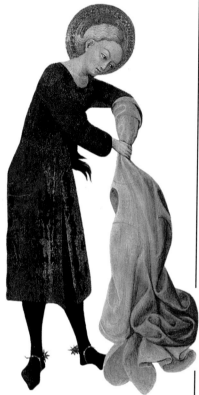

Ultramarine

THE KISS OF JUDAS
Giotto; c.1305–6; 78¾ x 72¾ in (200 x 185 cm); fresco
Giotto uses yellow ochre for the voluminous robe of Judas Iscariot, the disciple who betrayed Jesus to his enemies with a kiss. This color not only attracts the eye to the focus of the composition, but is also associated with evil and, more specifically, betrayal and cowardice. The meaning of this color would have been clear to Renaissance viewers. Other shades of yellow were used to identify St. Peter (Lorenzo's altarpiece, p. 16) and St. Joseph (Lippi's *Adoration*, p. 17). In non-Christian cultures, yellow has different associations: it was worn by the Emperor in Imperial China, while to ancient Hebrews, the yellow of the chrysolite gem gave protection from envy.

Vermilion

THE CRUCIFIXION
Masaccio; 1426; 30¼ x 25¼ in (83 x 63 cm); tempera on panel
The startling red robe belongs to the grieving figure of Mary Magdalene. She was the holy woman who witnessed Christ's crucifixion and mopped his bleeding feet with her flowing hair. Her robe is the color of his blood – the blood of sacrifice and martyrdom. From ancient times onward, red has been associated with blood and life: Chinese "oxblood" red vases were once used in sacrificial rites. Ultramarine also plays an important role in the narrative, drawing attention to St. John the Evangelist's grieving gesture (on the right).

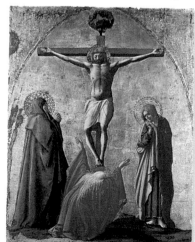

Egg tempera painting

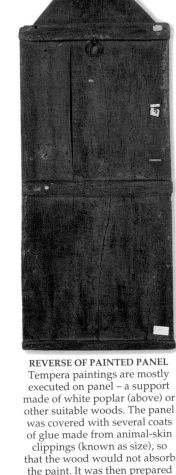

THE COLORS OF early panel paintings (from the 13th century to the late 15th century) are often beautifully preserved. This is because they are, in the main, painted in egg tempera – wet pigment (powdered color in water) bound in a medium of whole egg (sometimes just egg yolk). As the proteins in the egg harden, the colors acquire a sheen as soft as velvet and a skin as tough as shell. However, the watery content of the egg limits the range of pigments and the way they can be used. Because the water evaporates quickly, the paints begin to set almost immediately. This means that the colors are not at all easy to blend and have to be mixed beforehand in pure or simple combinations. Nor can the paint be applied thickly to create effects of texture, for it tends to shrink and crack. Colors must be painstakingly applied in thin, filmy layers, using light brushstrokes that will not lift the sticky paint lying underneath.

CENNINO'S HANDBOOK
"The Craftsman's Handbook" (c.1400; above), written by the Florentine painter Cennino Cennini, provides a detailed account of egg tempera techniques. These were based on a system of modeling (p. 62) figures in light and shade: pure color was used in the shadows, and lead white was added toward the highlights.

Ready-mixed egg tempera

Gesso (for grounds)

Egg yolk

Size (animal glue)

Whole egg

THE EGG MEDIUM
Tempera painting demands that the artist have a good knowledge of the materials. Cennino even recommends using the paler yolks of town hens so that they do not affect the clarity of the colors (he added that the redder yolks of country hens might be useful for painting swarthy or aged flesh tones).

REVERSE OF PAINTED PANEL
Tempera paintings are mostly executed on panel – a support made of white poplar (above) or other suitable woods. The panel was covered with several coats of glue made from animal-skin clippings (known as size), so that the wood would not absorb the paint. It was then prepared for painting with a brilliant white ground, made of gesso.

THE CORONATION OF THE VIRGIN
Lorenzo Monaco; c.1414; wings: 71½ x 41¼ in (181.6 x 104.8 cm); central panel: 85½ x 45½ in (217.2 x 115.6 cm); tempera on panel
This radiant altarpiece illustrates one of the main advantages of the Cennino system of modeling in white: the unnatural brightness of the colors. The altarpiece would have shone in its original dark church setting, with vivid pinks, yellows, greens, and blues easily holding their own against the metallic gold. Following the usual procedure, Lorenzo first completed the gilded areas, then the draperies, furnishings, and, finally, the flesh. The Virgin's white robe was once a deep pinkish mauve: Lorenzo used a red lake glaze (p. 22), which has faded away in the light.

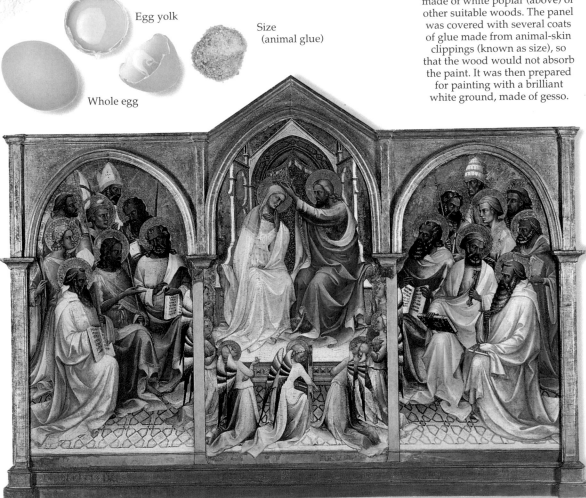

This *tondo* (Italian: "round painting") marks a transition between the old and new styles of coloring

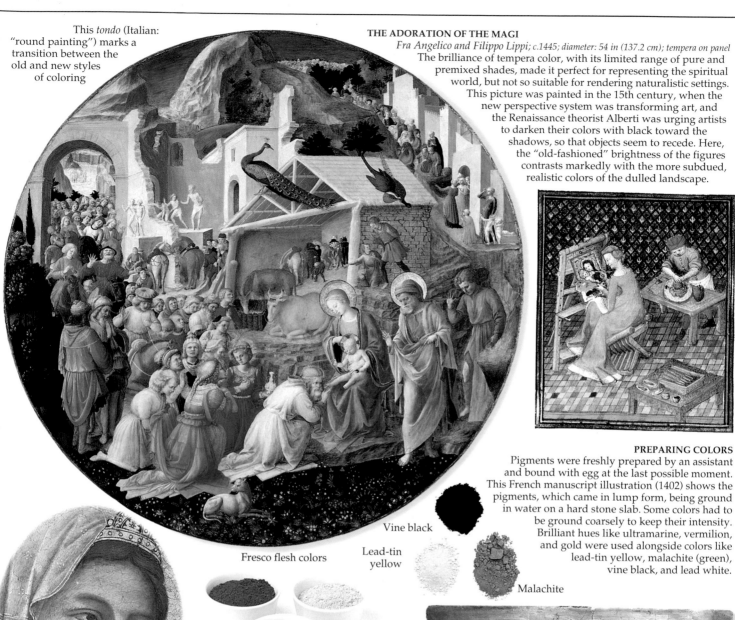

THE ADORATION OF THE MAGI

Fra Angelico and Filippo Lippi; c.1445; diameter: 54 in (137.2 cm); tempera on panel

The brilliance of tempera color, with its limited range of pure and premixed shades, made it perfect for representing the spiritual world, but not so suitable for rendering naturalistic settings. This picture was painted in the 15th century, when the new perspective system was transforming art, and the Renaissance theorist Alberti was urging artists to darken their colors with black toward the shadows, so that objects seem to recede. Here, the "old-fashioned" brightness of the figures contrasts markedly with the more subdued, realistic colors of the dulled landscape.

PREPARING COLORS

Pigments were freshly prepared by an assistant and bound with egg at the last possible moment. This French manuscript illustration (1402) shows the pigments, which came in lump form, being ground in water on a hard stone slab. Some colors had to be ground coarsely to keep their intensity. Brilliant hues like ultramarine, vermilion, and gold were used alongside colors like lead-tin yellow, malachite (green), vine black, and lead white.

Vine black

Lead-tin yellow

Malachite

Fresco flesh colors

Verdaccio

Cinabrese

Sinoper

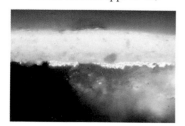

Detail of St. Catherine, from Duccio's *Maestà* (pp. 10–11)

GREEN FACES

This cross-section of flesh clearly shows the underpaint of green earth. In tempera paintings like the *Maestà* (detail, above), the top layer has worn down, leaving a greenish cast.

FLESH PAINTING

The only complex layering of color in tempera occurred in the areas of flesh. In this, tempera echoed fresco practice, in which an underpaint of *verdaccio* (a greenish mixture) was worked over with flesh colors: the pale red ochres – sinoper and cinabrese – mixed with lime white. In tempera, *terra verde* (Italian: "green earth") or *verdaccio* was used for the ground, followed by lead white tinted with vermilion.

VIRGIN AND CHILD WITH ST. ANDREW AND ST. PETER

Cima da Conegliano; c.1500; painted area: 18¾ x 15¼ in (47.8 x 38.9 cm); unfinished tempera and oil on panel

This unfinished painting stands at the crossroads of the old tempera and new oil techniques (pp. 22–23). Italian artists of this period often still used tempera for the initial modeling (see the figure on the left), because it is fast-drying. The underpainting was then glazed over with oil. Although oil soon replaced the old method, egg tempera is valued and used to this day.

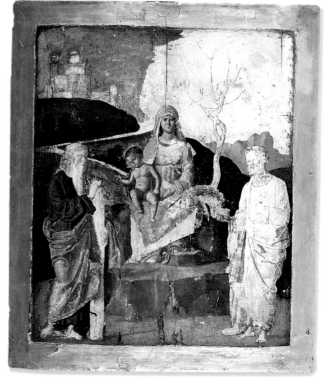

Color, light, and narrative

JUST AS INDIVIDUAL COLORS could be invested with symbolic meaning (pp. 14–15), so a particular "style" of coloring could be used to reflect the story or theme of a picture. This was largely a matter of decorum or appropriateness: that is, the style of coloring had to suit the nature of the subject painted. Leonardo da Vinci's dark, atmospheric manner (pp. 20–21) was particularly effective for dramatic or tragic subjects, while brilliant *cangiante* coloring (Italian: "changing") – where, in an area of unnaturally bright color, hues shift from one color to another across the surface – was often used for supernatural revelations. Piero della Francesca (c.1410/20–92) chose a limited range of colors to give his complex narratives clarity. For naturalistic subjects, the "harmonious" style of subtly blended tones was considered to be a judicious choice.

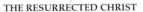

SUPERNATURAL COLOR
The popular German painter Matthias Grünewald (c.1460–1528) was renowned for the dynamism of his coloring. In his *Resurrected Christ* (below right), Christ – traditionally dark-haired and bearded – is transformed into a golden-haired figure with glowing red eyes. In this detail, his face dissolves in a blaze of light – from which his features emerge in all their dazzling beauty.

THE RESURRECTED CHRIST
Matthias Grünewald; c.1510–15; right-hand panel of triptych: 106 in x 56¼ in (269 x 143 cm); oil on panel
This panel from the Isenheim altarpiece in Germany, illustrating the joy of Christ's resurrection, vividly contrasts with Grünewald's darkly expressive scene of crucifixion (far left). Christ's skin is white, free of all taints of sin and suffering, apart from the gleaming red stigmata (marks left by the nails of his crucifixion). He trails a radiant *cangiante* cloth: the white is "shot" through with blue, in the manner of shot silk (p. 62), which miraculously changes to blazing hues of rose, orange, and pure yellow. These colors are echoed in the halo of light around Christ's head. Below, the earthbound soldiers, painted in duller earth colors, stumble and flounder, blinded by the light.

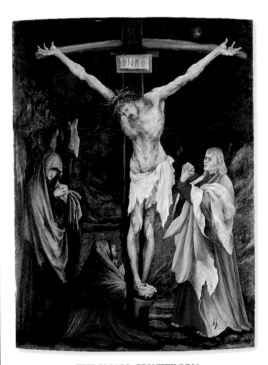

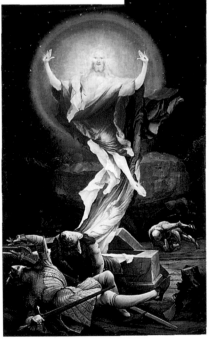

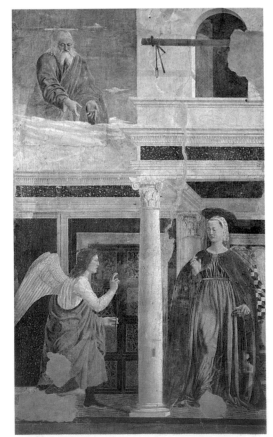

THE SMALL CRUCIFIXION
Matthias Grünewald; c.1511/20; 24¼ x 18¼ in (61.3 x 46 cm); oil on panel
Somber colors – gangrenous greens, midnight blues, and deep reds – convey the anguish of the crucifixion. In the livid light, Christ's pale green, bloodless figure is exposed in all its agony. His mother's blackened garments express the intensity of her grief, while Mary Magdalene's robe forms a pool of blood red.

THE ANNUNCIATION
Piero della Francesca; c.1455; 129½ x 76 in (329 x 193 cm); fresco
This fresco is part of a cycle illustrating the Legend of the True Cross – the cross of Christ's crucifixion. Piero alludes to the cross structurally and symbolically, using a restrained palette of rose, dark green, white, brown, and blue that emphasizes the different levels of the narrative.
The fresco is divided into a Latin cross, formed by the architecture: the upright of the white pillar and "arms" of rose and green marble. In the spaces between, the monumental figures of God and the Virgin echo each other in rose and blue, while the beam across the open window is mirrored by the brown cross-beams of the door below – both of which refer symbolically to the cross.

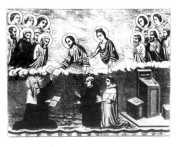

BRIDGET'S VISIONS
Grünewald was greatly inspired by the mystical Revelations of St. Bridget of Sweden, a text of stark and visionary intensity. This engraving is after a miniature in a 14th-century edition.

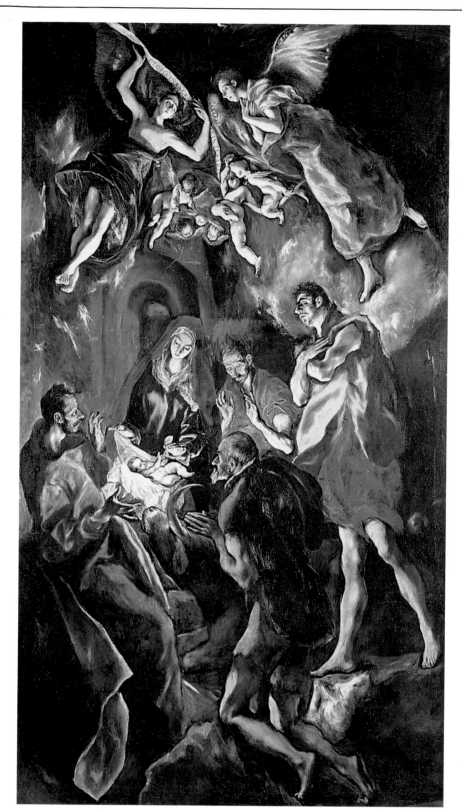

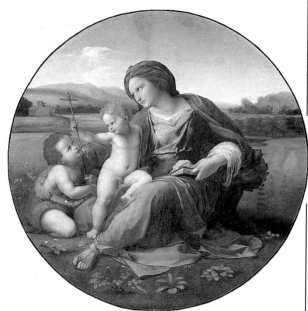

THE ALBA MADONNA
Raphael; c.1510; diameter: 37¼ in (94.5 cm);
oil on panel, transferred to canvas
Raphael (1483–1520), a master of different styles of coloring, chose a low key harmony of tones (further muted by a layer of yellowed varnish) for this gentle theme. Red and ultramarine are subdued to blend the Madonna with the soft landscape colors, for this is the Madonna of Humility, who is always shown seated on bare ground.

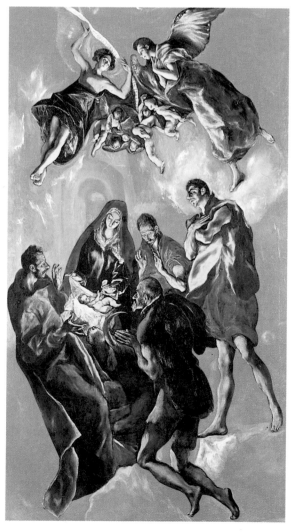

THE ADORATION OF THE SHEPHERDS
El Greco; 1612–14; 126 x 70¾ in (319 x 180 cm); oil on canvas
El Greco painted this ecstatic scene for his burial vault in the church of San Domingo el Antiguo in Toledo, Spain. He chose to set the scene in the dark cave setting mentioned in the early Book of James, but filled it with silvery supernatural light. As in St. Bridget's vision, this radiance emanates from the Christ child, illuminating the pale flesh tones and deep, saturated colors of the draperies of the figures. It also picks out the sun-baked features of the elderly shepherd kneeling in the foreground, who is thought to be a self-portrait of the artist.

MYSTICAL UNION
The colors of the draperies – red, orange, blue, gold, and green – form two glowing circles around the newborn Christ: the earthly sphere, represented by Mary, Joseph, and the shepherds; and the angelic sphere, in a halo of brightness above. By spiraling colors upward in an inverted "S" shape, from the orange on the shoulder of the shepherd, the eye is drawn into the spiritual heart of the composition, where Heaven and Earth are joined.

Leonardo's naturalism

THE ITALIAN RENAISSANCE MASTER Leonardo da Vinci (1452–1519) applied his remarkable intellect to the science of vision, color, and light. By gaining universal insights from the tiniest details of nature, such as the colored veins in pebbles or the light on windblown leaves, he created a new ideal of naturalistic color. He developed *chiaroscuro* – a method of painting using light and shadow (pp. 30–31) – whereby forms suffused in light seem to emerge in three dimensions from darkness. The more subtle *sfumato* (Italian: "smoky") technique, in which colors and contours are softened by smoky shadows, was his own invention. In landscape backgrounds, Leonardo practiced his "aerial" perspective (p. 24), imitating the way nature's hues become bluer over distance, as they penetrate atmospheric mists and vapors.

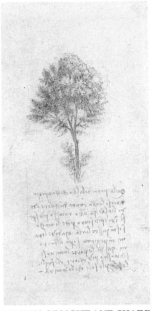

Glass for "considering color mixtures"

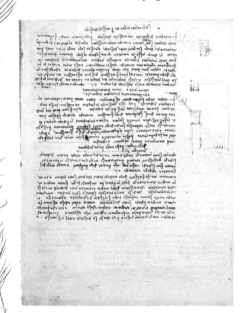

THE RAINBOW COLORS OF NATURE
Leonardo enthusiastically explored the colors of the rainbow in his notebooks (left). Its myriad hues were observed in bubbles of water, peacock feathers, "the roots of turnips kept in stagnant waters" – surrounded by rainbows of reflected light – and "antique glass found underground." As a practical guide to seeing the infinite color mixtures in nature, he suggested looking at countryside through pieces of colored glass, to see which of nature's colors would be "impaired" or "improved" by blending. Yellow and green glass were found to enhance color the most.

STUDIES OF LIGHT AND SHADE
Leonardo stated that "the scientific and true principles of painting first establish what is a shaded body [form], and what is light." He made exhaustive studies of the effects of sunlight and shadow on the colors of trees and leaves (above), from which he formulated general rules. He took into account the thickness of the branching, the dappling effect of shadow, and even the shape of the leaf itself.

GINEVRA DE' BENCI
Leonardo da Vinci; c.1474; 15¼ x 14½ in (38.8 x 36.7 cm); oil on panel
In this early portrait, Leonardo uses *chiaroscuro* to create a sense of relief that rivals the roundness of sculpture – the figure seems to project from the picture surface. He also reveals the painterly contrasts between smooth, luminous flesh, soft, lustrous curls, and dark, spiky juniper leaves. Brilliant colors are banished, for Leonardo believed that a painting "may be adorned with ugly colors, and yet astonish those who contemplate it, through the appearance of relief."

SOFTENED LANDSCAPE
This landscape detail from *Ginevra* shows Leonardo exploring Flemish advances in oil technique (p. 22). The shifts in color – created by translucent glazes – enhance the effect of distance, the palest blue being farthest away.

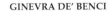

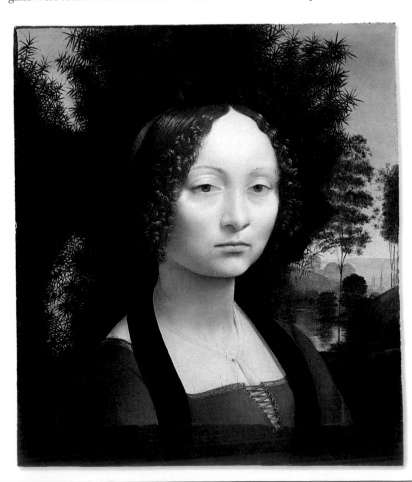

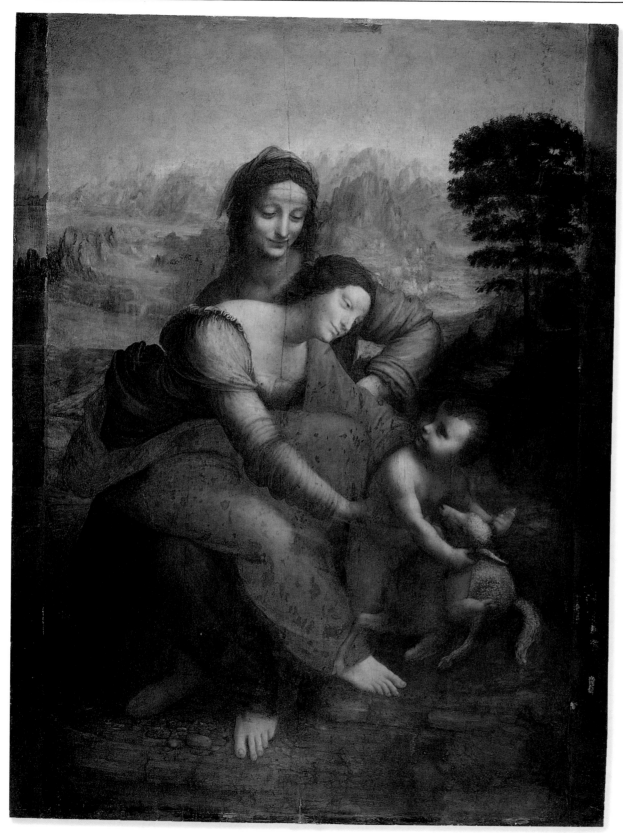

TRANSPARENT VEILS
Leonardo's painting shows his concern with transparency. Thin glazes cast a "veil" of atmosphere over the landscape; and painted veils adorn St. Anne's forehead and reveal the Virgin's bare arm. The dark area in the foreground may have once been a clear pool.

ULTRAMARINE SICKNESS
The strange, milky flatness of the blue robe worn by the Virgin is possibly due to "ultramarine sickness." This is caused when the pigment comes into contact with an acid, from any source, and loses its color entirely.

COLORED PEBBLES
Small colored pebbles, like those at St. Anne's feet, were of special interest to Leonardo. From their patterned formations of colored minerals, he learned about larger geological structures and the intricacy of natural color harmonies.

DOMINATING BROWN
A strong, brownish underpainting, often consisting of bitumen brown (below), gave a sculptural foundation of light and shade that Leonardo allowed to show through his colors. Most other dark brown tones are due to the browning of copper-based greens, like verdigris (below), a problem that the artist wrote of in his notebooks.

The Virgin, Infant Jesus, and St. Anne

LEONARDO DA VINCI *after c.1507; 66¼ x 51¼ in (168 x 130 cm); oil on canvas*
This late painting is a lovely example of Leonardo's delicate *sfumato* technique. Shadows are blurred in a mist of smoky color and outlines have disappeared. The expressions on the faces hover between soft light and shadow, while the figures in this gentle scene fuse together in natural harmony and seem to move and breathe. Even the shifts of color in the mysterious, rocky landscape are virtually imperceptible.

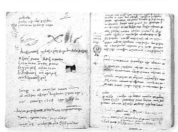

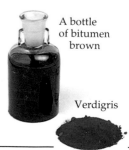

A bottle of bitumen brown

Verdigris

Coloring in oils

THE REFINEMENT OF OIL PAINTING in the early 15th century opened up an almost unlimited range of color possibilities. In this technique, the powdered pigment is mixed with a slow-drying oil – such as linseed or walnut – that absorbs oxygen from the air, forming a transparent skin that locks the color in. This means that oil paint can be built up in many layers, and applied opaquely (thickly, so that light cannot penetrate it), semitransparently, or in transparent glazes (usually thinned with glossy turpentine or resins). Because the oil dries slowly, the "edges" of colors can also be blended and fused easily. Early on, artists exploited the smooth transparency of glazes, which allow light from a luminous underlayer to shine through. Colors could be modified simply by varying the underpaint, transparency, or order of layers: in one painting only three or four pigments were used to create over 20 different shades of red and pink! Later, artists began to explore the rich textural possibilities of oil paint in an increasingly free and personal manner.

Walnut oil **Linseed oil**

Walnuts

THE OIL MEDIUM
The oils most frequently used by the Old Masters were linseed and walnut. These dry slowly – unlike olive oil, for instance, which never dries – and form a flexible surface. Linseed was particularly valued by van Eyck (below right) for the smooth, jewel-like brilliance it gave to colors. Walnut oil is thinner (Leonardo suggested that it should be left in the sun to thicken), but it does not yellow as much as linseed – oils often turn yellow or brown with age.

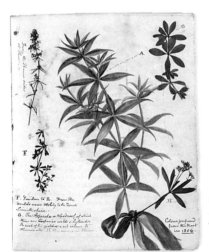

LAKE PIGMENTS
Lake pigments – organic inklike dyes deposited in a powder base, such as chalk (p. 62) – were often used as oil glazes, since, when mixed with a binding medium, they become translucent. Madder lake is a lovely transparent red made from the roots of the madder plant. Carmine, from crushed cochineal insects, makes an exquisite (if perishable) crimson glaze. Yellow lakes, derived from berries, fade in oil and are best avoided.

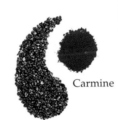

Carmine

Cochineal insects

Madder roots from the madder plant (illustration, far left)

Yellow lake

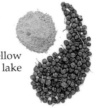

Buckthorn berries

WET-IN-WET
These close-up details are from van Eyck's *Annunciation* (far right), but after its 1992–93 cleaning. The threads in the Angel Gabriel's green brocade robe were skillfully stroked across the green underlayer while it was wet.

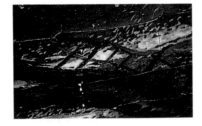

Gabriel's green robe (after cleaning)

RICH GLAZING
This detail from the Angel Gabriel's red velvet mantle shows how van Eyck uses red glaze over a full-bodied opaque underpaint to suggest the richness and texture of the fabric. Small cracks in the paint reveal the white ground beneath.

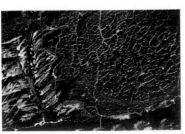

Gabriel's red mantle (after cleaning)

THE ANNUNCIATION
Jan van Eyck; c.1434–36;
35½ x 14 in (90.2 x 34.1 cm);
oil on canvas, transferred from panel
In his own lifetime, the Flemish painter Jan van Eyck (c.1390–1441) was celebrated as "the inventor of oil painting" – although drying oils had been used since at least the 8th century. However, van Eyck did develop the technique to an astonishing degree, exploiting the optical properties of superimposed layers of glazes to create an endless variety of subtle light effects. Working on a reflective white ground, he applied glassy transparent layers so that the light would penetrate and bounce back off the white to the eye. For the shadows, he used multiple layers of thicker glaze to deepen and enrich the colors, rather than muddying them with black.

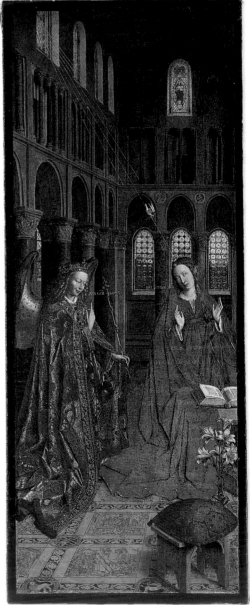

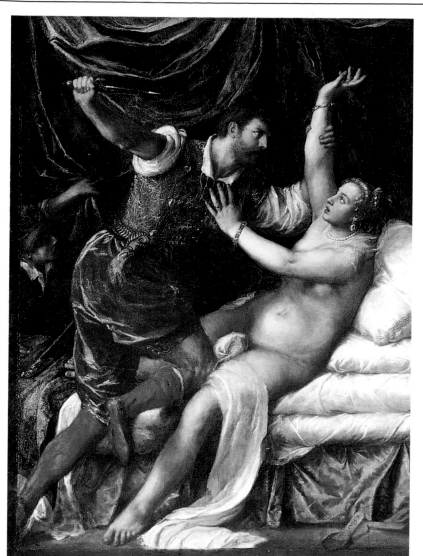

TARQUIN AND LUCRETIA
*Titian; 1568–76; 71¾ x 55 in
(182 x 140 cm); oil on canvas*
The great Venetian painter Titian
(c.1487–1576) vigorously exploited
the new freedom and flexibility of
the oil technique. He described this
late picture, showing the brutal rape
of Lucretia by the King of Rome,
Tarquin, as the product of much
"labor and artifice." Analysis of
the painting has shown that Titian
changed both the coloring and
composition as he worked (right),
and made other alterations over the
three years in which it was kept in
his studio. The colors are applied
in incredibly complex layers, often
including contrasting hues (p. 39).
In the reddish-green curtain, for
example, blue and green mingle in
the shadows. Titian was never afraid
to "dirty" his colors, as he put it,
to produce richer natural effects.

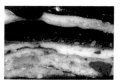

THE COUNTERPANE
In this cross-section, the
change from orange-red
to green seems to be
due to changes in the
color scheme made by
Titian as he painted.

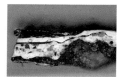

TARQUIN'S BREECHES
The deep red is built up
in layers: red lead, thick
pink and white impasto
(p. 62), and red glazes.

X-RAY VISION
This X-ray enables
us to look beneath the
surface of the painting
(the lead in Titian's
pigments absorbs the
rays). It reveals the
changes made by Titian
in the composition –
most obviously the
shift in position of
Tarquin's dagger
and right arm.

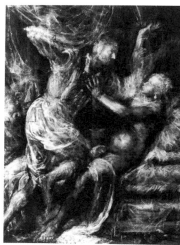

Lead white
pigment
shows up
in X-rays

MINERVA PROTECTS PAX FROM MARS (PEACE AND WAR)
*Peter Paul Rubens; 1629–30; 80 x
117¼ in (203.5 x 298 cm); oil on canvas*
The works of the 17th-century
master Rubens (1577–1640) reveal
the full potential of oil painting.
The luminosity and soft fluidity
of color were thought to be due to
the use of lustrous resins, although
they are now attributed to Rubens's
dazzling painting skills. He uses
fresh and simple color mixtures,
painting his shadows thinly so
that he does not dull their
transparency and warmth.

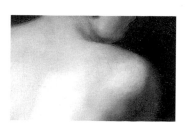

COLORED SHADOWS
In the flesh, warm glazes are
interspersed with strokes of pale
gray, blue, and green to suggest
the colored lights in the shadows.

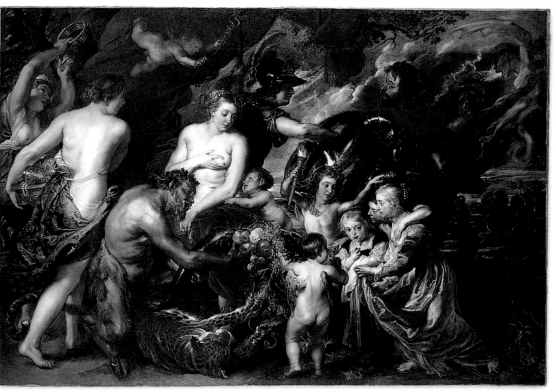

Color and space

Color and light are powerful tools in the creation of a sense of space. Tones can be gradually shifted from dark to pale, creating subtle gradations of brightness that the eye follows into the distance. The nature of color itself can be exploited – reds tend to advance and blues tend to recede. These effects have been explained by optical science (p. 33). But our perception of space and depth in landscape is also influenced by an external phenomenon: in nature, colors lose their intensity and distinctness at a distance because of the increasing body of air or "atmosphere" through which they are seen. The short wavelengths of blue light (p. 6) travel through this veil of air more easily than the longer wavelengths of red, which is why color appears paler and bluer toward the horizon. The coloristic device that mimics these effects is known as aerial or atmospheric perspective.

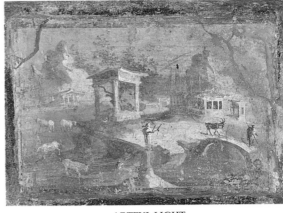

ARTFUL LIGHT
In this idyllic Pompeian landscape, from the mid-1st century A.D., light enters from the side, illuminating the golden facades of shrines and temples, and dissolving distant forms in hazy violet-gray shadow. The impression of light and depth is enhanced by the use of green and brown – local colors (p. 62) – in the foreground, as opposed to the unreal, pastel hues of the background.

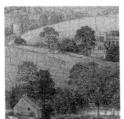

Detail of blue landscape

THE REST ON THE FLIGHT INTO EGYPT
Gerard David; c.1510; 16½ x 16¼ in (41.9 x 42.2 cm); oil on panel
This landscape by Gerard David (c.1460–1523) moves in gentle steps from the warm grays and ochres of the foreground rocks to a pale lemon-green clearing, where Joseph is busy knocking down chestnuts. The more abrupt transition to the cool blues of the distant landscape (created by lead white tinted with azurite; detail, left) is masked by dark bushes.

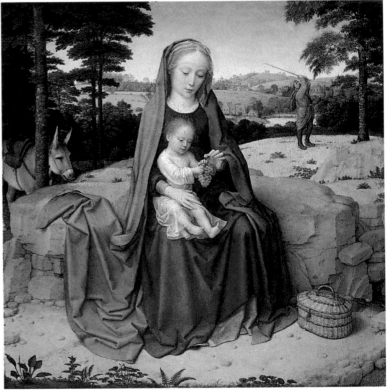

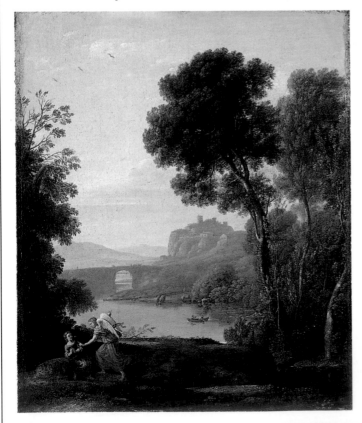

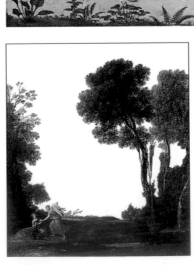

LANDSCAPE WITH HAGAR AND THE ANGEL
Claude Lorrain; 1646; 20¾ x 17¼ in (52.7 x 43.8 cm); oil on canvas, mounted on panel
Claude Lorrain (1600–82) developed a foolproof formula for creating the type of landscape that it seemed the viewer could walk through. The effect was created by framing the landscape with a dark foreground and tall trees that acted like stage wings (left). These wings open onto a luminous middle distance, with a stretch of water leading the eye back into space. The subtle color transitions follow the rules of aerial perspective, moving from a misty townscape to pale, faraway hills.

THE DOGANA AND SANTA MARIA DELLA SALUTE

J.M.W. Turner; c.1843; 24½ x 36¾ in (62 x 93 cm); oil on canvas

J.M.W. Turner (1775–1851) was fascinated by diffused sunlight – particularly at dawn – as can be seen in this radiant Venetian view. In Venice, Turner could use his favored palette of white, luminous yellows, pinks, blues, and grays to create a shimmering vision of light and space – without having to touch the "nasty" greens he abhorred. The golden mass of the landing jetty and the dark diagonal of the moored gondolas lead the eye into a floating space that is only defined in our imagination. Its glassy grayness is brought to life by hints of pure color.

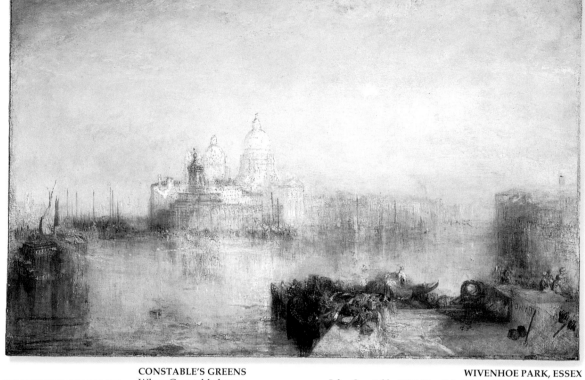

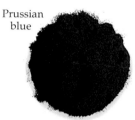

Prussian blue

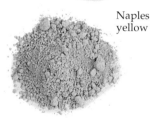

Naples yellow

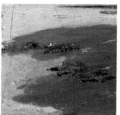

Detail of green landscape

CONSTABLE'S GREENS

When Constable began painting, the green pigments available were dull and disappointing (the bright emerald green only appeared in 1814), so he created his green color mixtures from Prussian blue and Naples yellow (far left).

WIVENHOE PARK, ESSEX

John Constable; 1816; 22 x 40 in (56.1 x 101.2 cm); oil on canvas

In contrast to Turner, John Constable (1776–1837) used a great variety of greens to create this exceptionally spacious landscape. Constable was anxious to suggest space through natural colors like grass green, rather than employing the artificial range of hues used in aerial perspective, which usually ranged from mellow reddish browns to silvery pale blues. Nevertheless, his khaki foreground, warmed by small accents of red, is still close to the brown traditionally used by artists such as Claude (far left), while blues are visible in the sunlit greens of the background.

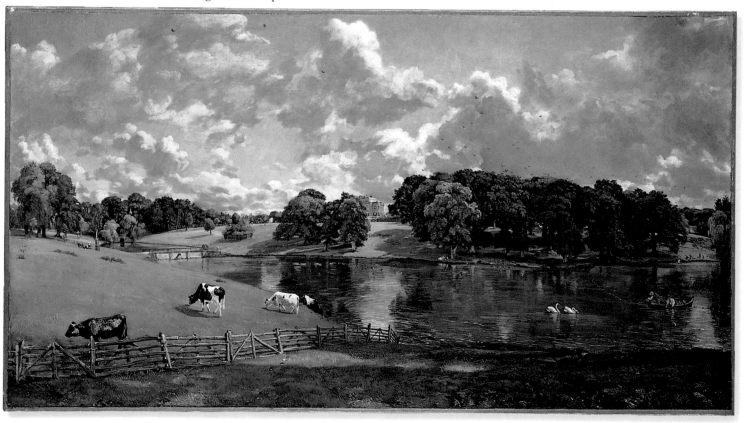

The Venetian School

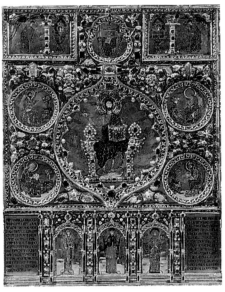

THE VENETIAN PAINTERS of the 16th century were renowned for their dazzling way with color. While their fellow countrymen in Tuscany continued to paint in bright colors isolated by firm outlines, the Venetians chose to confine themselves to a range of exceptionally rich and pure pigments, applied in blended patches. The quality of their colors was largely due to Venice's position as a leading maritime port. Built on a shimmering lagoon, she traded in luxury goods, importing cargoes of exotic spices, rich silks, jewelry, scents, and new dyes and pigments from the Eastern Mediterranean. While artists from all over Italy sent to Venice for foreign pigments, the Venetians received them first and made their novelty into a specialty. But it was the way that they handled these colors that set the Venetian painters apart. As well as delighting in the brilliance of the pigments themselves, they subtly balanced, mixed, and interwove them in the interests of "truth" and harmony, using color saturation and brightness to suggest natural light effects. As a consequence, the figures and settings merge in a haze of light and atmosphere.

BIRD'S-EYE VIEW OF VENICE
Venice's position as "queen of the sea," with a large Mediterranean empire (stretching from Istria, to Crete and Cyprus), made her the richest and most powerful city in Italy in the 16th century. The quality of her imported goods was unrivaled: the ultramarine used by the leading Venetian painter of the time, Titian (below), is of the highest purity and intensity.

THE PALACE OF GOLD
Venice's passion for color and precious materials was reflected in her architecture. The Byzantine *Pala d'Oro* (Italian: "Palace of Gold") was encrusted with gold, enamelwork, and jewels: this section from the *Pala d'Oro* (1105) shows Christ in judgment. Other palaces were adorned with colored marbles or frescoes. "He that will row through the Grand Canal," wrote a visiting Englishman, "shall see [houses] more like the dwellings of princes than private men."

DANAE
Titian; 1553; 50¼ x 70 in (127.5 x 178 cm); oil on canvas
This late work by Titian – depicting the rape of Danaë by the god Jupiter (in the form of a shower of gold) – shows the vigorous originality of his handling of the brush. Strokes of different colors are placed side by side. They blend together only when they are viewed at a distance. Varieties of paint texture interact with the weave of the canvas to emphasize the contrasts between the energetic shower (detail, below), the golden-skinned Danaë, and the mottled body of the old attendant.

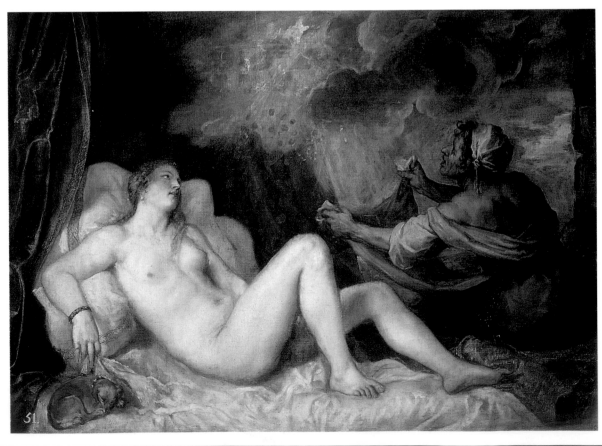

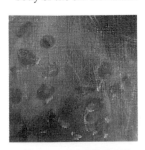

"Shower of gold" detail

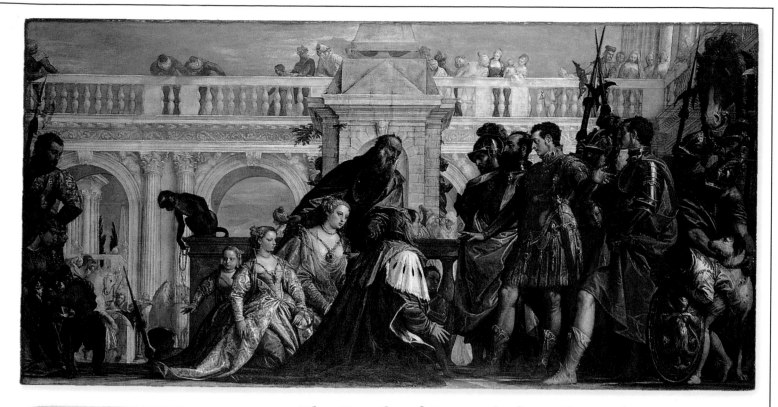

The Family of Darius before Alexander

PAOLO VERONESE *c.1570s; 93 x 187 in (236.2 x 474.9 cm); oil on canvas*

Paolo Veronese (c.1528–88) was the master of the Venetian "narrative" – large canvases that decorated walls in much the same way as fresco. Since they were painted in oil, there were no color limitations, but Venetian artists chose to limit their palette to a small number of hues. Veronese delighted in creating unusual, blended color mixtures ("broken" colors) from this range. His famous Veronese green (above) is created from a solid green underpaint (lead-tin yellow, verdigris, and a little malachite) with a copper resinate glaze.

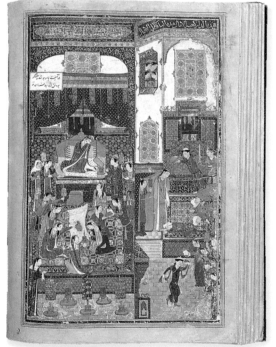

EASTERN PIGMENTS
The Venetians borrowed two beautiful pigments from manuscript painters of the East: realgar (orange-red) and orpiment (yellow). These regularly appear in Persian manuscript illuminations, such as this one, and surface in Venetian painting in the 1490s. Realgar provided the Italians with the first true orange (previously they had mixed red and yellow), and the two pigments combined produced glorious reddish golds.

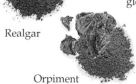

Realgar

Orpiment

POISONOUS PIGMENTS
Realgar (arsenic sulfide) and orpiment (yellow arsenic trisulfide) are two of the most poisonous pigments.

COSMETIC COLOR
Painters often heightened the reds of flesh tones (detail, right) with vermilion, or glazes made from red lakes such as madder or brazilwood (far right). This partly reflects the liberal use of rouge by Venetian women; rouge was made from brazilwood or dragon's blood (a tree resin). As an artistic practice, it was frowned upon by Vasari, the Renaissance art historian, who complained that it "falsifies the freshness of living flesh."

Verona green

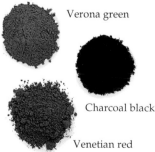

Charcoal black

Venetian red

LOCAL RESOURCES
Painters also valued relatively dull local colors, such as green earth (from Verona), charcoal black, and Venetian red.

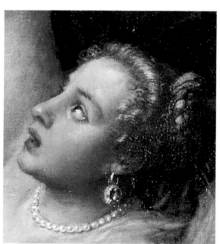

Detail from Titian's *Tarquin and Lucretia* (p. 23)

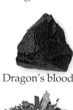

Dragon's blood

Brazilwood

Madder

THE DYER'S TRADE
Venice was a major center of wool and silk dyeing. New colors were continually being developed, along with more permanent fixatives. People clothed themselves in a variety of shades, which often echoed the broken colors of Venetian painting: *flammeo* (Italian: "flame"), for example, hovered between orange and gold.

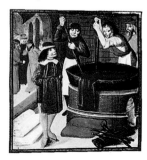

The restoration of color

THE RECENT CLEANING of the frescoes by Michelangelo (1475–1564) in the Sistine Chapel in Rome has caused widespread controversy over the true colors of Old Master paintings. Original colors are often obscured by the grime of centuries, and are sometimes even completely distorted by "repaints," where restorers of the past have tried to match the colors to the tastes of their own times. In the 19th century, collectors liked their pictures to have the warm, dark tones of a Rembrandt (p. 31): *The Feast of the Gods*, by the Venetian masters Giovanni Bellini (c.1430/40–1516) and Titian, was overpainted where it had been damaged, and given a layer of varnish – its yellowing later subdued the colors further. Now, restorers try to re-create the original appearance of a painting, using the latest technology to analyze the pigments and binding media.

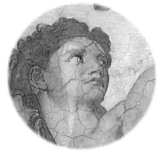

MICHELANGELO'S EVE
This unrestored detail of Eve from the Sistine Ceiling shows that animal glue was brushed over the fresco, darkening the colors. A triangular area has been missed, revealing the original, brighter hues.

THE LIBYAN SIBYL
Michelangelo; c.1508; fresco; detail of the Sistine Ceiling
When Michelangelo's restored Sistine Ceiling was revealed, it caused a critical uproar. Before cleaning, the dusky colors (left) were described as "sculptural" rather than painterly, echoing the brooding, "melancholy" temperament of the artist. After cleaning, these ideas had to be abandoned. As the restored *Libyan Sibyl* (far left) shows, Michelangelo was not only a wonderful colorist, but also a pioneer in this field. Never before had *cangiante* coloring (p. 18) been used on this scale. The dynamic, shot hues (p. 62) of the draperies give the figures a spiritual energy and beauty, in keeping with the optimistic spirit of Renaissance Christianity.

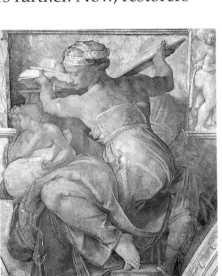

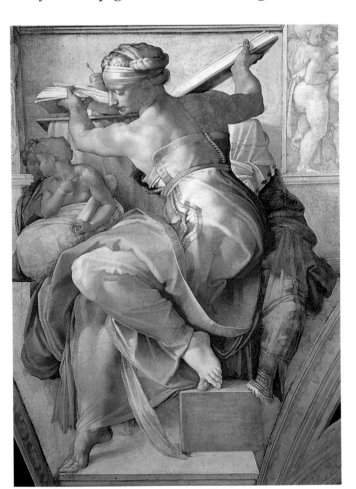

Michelangelo's *Libyan Sibyl*, after the restoration of the Sistine Ceiling

THE FEAST OF THE GODS
Giovanni Bellini and Titian; 1514/1529;
67 x 74 in (170.2 x 188 cm); oil on canvas; before restoration
In 1568, Vasari described this painting as "one of the most beautiful works that Giovanni Bellini ever created." Vasari added: "Unable to carry through this work because he, Bellini, was old, Titian was summoned, since he was better than all others, so that he might bring it to completion." X-rays of the painting from the 1950s confirm that Titian had substantially repainted the landscape. The discolored resin varnish was only removed in 1985, revealing glorious Venetian color.

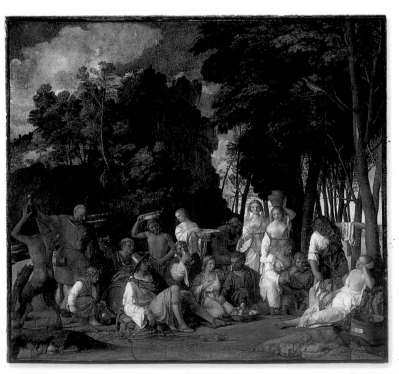

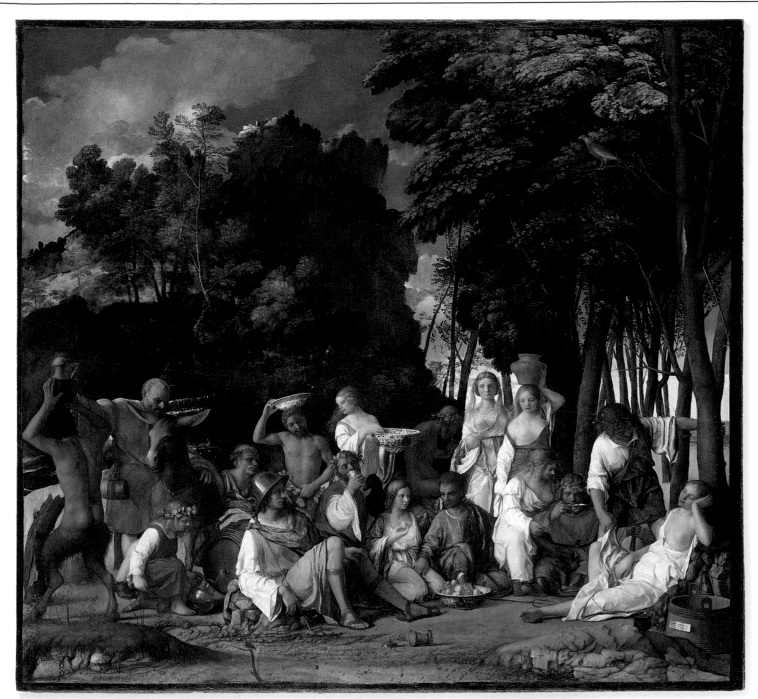

The Feast of the Gods

BELLINI AND TITIAN *as left; after restoration*
When the layer of varnish was stripped away, it was found that, in the early 19th century, all of the draperies of the figures had been toned down. Some of the foliage had also been thickly overpainted, to give it the golden glow so admired at the time. Few were prepared for the brilliance and variety of the colors that emerged. The brooding landscape was transformed into a sunlit glade, filled with air and movement, while the gods appeared in an array of rich draperies. Rose pinks, blues, oranges, and other bright shades appear alongside shot hues, like those of the splendid crimson and pale turquoise tunic, worn by the helmeted god, Mercury.

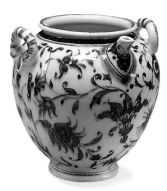

BLUE-AND-WHITE PORCELAIN
The restoration has revealed the delicate detail and luster of the Chinese porcelain (similar to this 16th-century Medici ware), held by the satyr and nymph.

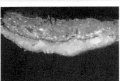

SILENUS'S DRAPERY
These cross-sections of paint samples were removed during cleaning. Here, thin orange-red ochre paint lies over the realgar and orpiment of Silenus's robe (figure on left).

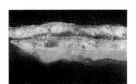

CYBELE'S DRESS
Cybele's salmon pink dress (center) is composed of lead white, vermilion, and red lake. There are crimson glazes in the shadowy folds, with touches of yellow in the lights.

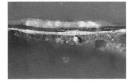

PRIAPUS'S DRAPERY
This sample from Priapus's shot drapery (second figure from right), shows varnish on an opaque red-orange layer (vermilion with iron oxides), over a transparent green.

Chiaroscuro: light and shadow

*C*HIAROSCURO – LITERALLY "BRIGHT-DARK" (Italian) – was an effect, pioneered by Leonardo da Vinci (pp. 20–21), which focused on dramatic contrasts of light and shade. While Leonardo used it primarily to model forms, painters like the Italian Caravaggio (c.1571/2–1610) exploited it in the interests of narrative and spiritual impact, thrusting his figures into the spotlight and allowing the deep shadows to mold and engulf their forms and features. Such daring coloristic effects can be compared to the manipulative lighting of vintage Hollywood movies. Caravaggio's influence was enormous. In the 17th century, Georges de La Tour (1593–1652) used the exaggerated *tenebroso* (Italian: "dark") technique of Caravaggio's later years to create images of stillness, while Rembrandt (1606–69) explored the painterly drama of light and shadow. Later, Edouard Manet (1832–83) was inspired by the pure contrast of light and dark tones.

CANDLELIGHT
Some artists painted by candlelight to achieve a *chiaroscuro* effect, while others worked by the "red" of a blazing fire.

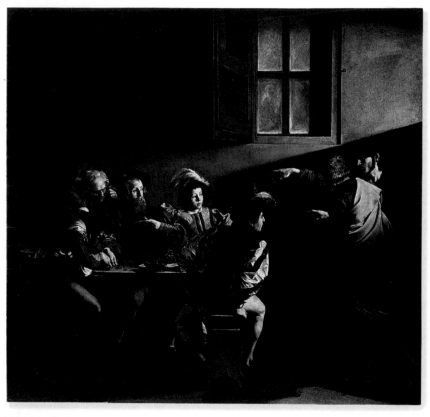

THE CALLING OF ST. MATTHEW
Caravaggio; c.1597–98; 126¾ x 133¾ in (322 x 340 cm); oil on canvas
This startling scene was painted for the Contarelli Chapel in the church of San Luigi dei Francesi in Rome. The chapel is very dark, but Caravaggio avoided the brilliant hues favored by his contemporaries, choosing a limited palette of blacks, blues, and whites, and using warm earth colors that would glow in the chapel's gloom. One fellow painter, Carracci, commented that Caravaggio "ground flesh" to make his earth pigments. Here, Matthew (the tax gatherer) and his friends are seated at a tavern table, their rich costumes contrasting with the poor garments of two barefoot figures on the right. The shrouded, enigmatic figure of Christ is identified by his strong gesture, illuminated by a dramatic shaft of light from the side.

OUT OF DARKNESS
The light on the figures of Christ and St. Peter (detail, right) gains its amazing spiritual power from the impenetrable black shadow that throws Christ's face and hand into sharp relief and bites into their forms. The flesh is shadowed – no match for the brilliantly illuminated face of Matthew's young companion – but, against the black, it glows with a simmering intensity.

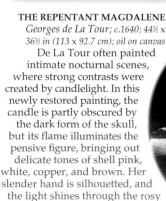

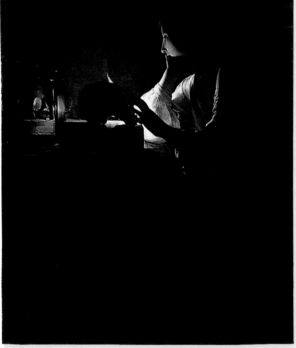

THE REPENTANT MAGDALENE
Georges de La Tour; c.1640; 44½ x 36½ in (113 x 92.7 cm); oil on canvas
De La Tour often painted intimate nocturnal scenes, where strong contrasts were created by candlelight. In this newly restored painting, the candle is partly obscured by the dark form of the skull, but its flame illuminates the pensive figure, bringing out delicate tones of shell pink, white, copper, and brown. Her slender hand is silhouetted, and the light shines through the rosy flesh of her fingers (detail, right).

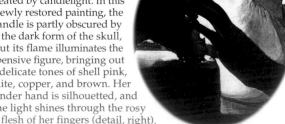

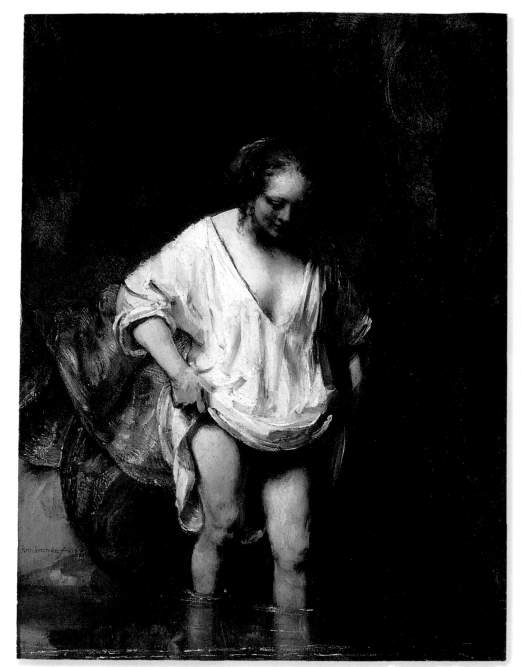

A WOMAN BATHING IN A STREAM

*Rembrandt; 1654; 24¼ x 18½ in
(61.8 x 47 cm); oil on panel*

This sensual painting was probably made for Rembrandt's private enjoyment. The direct application of paint shows particularly clearly how Rembrandt achieved his rich light effects. The panel is primed (p. 62) with a warm yellow-brown – visible in the unpainted strip on the lower curve of the woman's shift – that glows through the pigments. It is combined with wonderfully thick strokes of white and gray in the shift, and the yellow and orange ochres of the robe, to suggest light and texture. The shadows are described by dark tones, as well as alternating "warm" and "cool" colors; reddish tones give an impression of warmth, while bluer tones seem cool (p. 62). Here, they are used to give the flesh a sense of roundness.

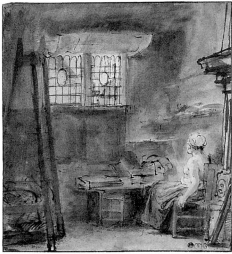

A MODEL IN THE ARTIST'S STUDIO

The effect of studio lighting on color was a major consideration. In this drawing by Rembrandt (c.1655), the studio window is fitted with a canopy so that the artist can control the light. Rembrandt's contemporary, Sandrart, observed that some studios were so filled with sunshine that the colors became "diminished and confused." He recommended north-facing windows with blinds or adjustable shutters to give a "richness of shadow and reflection."

Burnt umber   Burnt sienna   Spanish brown

REMBRANDT'S PALETTE

Rembrandt's palette was rich in earth pigments – ochres, umbers, and siennas. These were cheap, stable, and could be used raw, or roasted (burnt) to give richer or warmer shades, before mixing with oil.

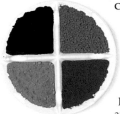

CREATING BLACK

Manet's "lively" blacks have been found to include bright colors – ivory black was even mixed with red lake, cobalt blue, and orange (left).

STILL LIFE WITH MELON AND PEACHES

Edouard Manet; c.1866; 27¼ x 36¼ in (69 x 92.2 cm); oil on canvas

The great 19th-century master Manet chose a stark frontal lighting as opposed to the lighting from the side that was favored by so many of his predecessors (far left).

This head-on approach flattens the forms, allowing Manet to omit the in between tones of traditional *chiaroscuro* and paint in unmodulated areas of lights and darks. He explained his effects: "Don't bother about the background. Look for the values. When you look [at a still life], when you want to render it as you see it ... you don't see the stripes on the wallpaper."

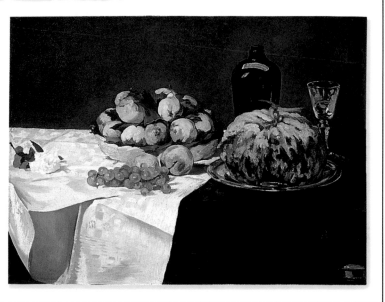

Painting with light

THE DUTCH PAINTER JAN VERMEER (1632–75) was fascinated by light and its painted effects: the luster of shiny surfaces, the highlights on skin and textured fabrics, and the depth of color in shadow. Like the French masters Jean-Baptiste Chardin (1699–1779) and Henri Fantin-Latour (1836–1904), Vermeer was intrigued by the effect of light on hue and tonal values (p. 7) – for example, the way blues lighten in dim daylight conditions, while reds appear particularly bright in intense light. All three painters sacrifice detail to light, describing the imperfect way we actually see. Chardin even blurs the face of his figure in *A Lady Taking Tea* to make sure that the viewer's eye roves naturally over the picture.

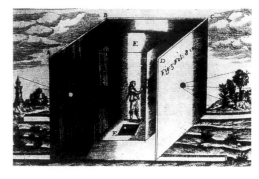

OPTICAL IMAGES
Vermeer's preoccupation with light, color, and texture led to his use of a room-type "camera obscura" (above). The camera – a darkened cubicle with a pinhole, through which light entered – produced a condensed image of the subject to be painted on a screen or wall. The image appeared in miniature: the effects of light and shade were dramatically contrasted, while colors took on a crystalline clarity and intensity.

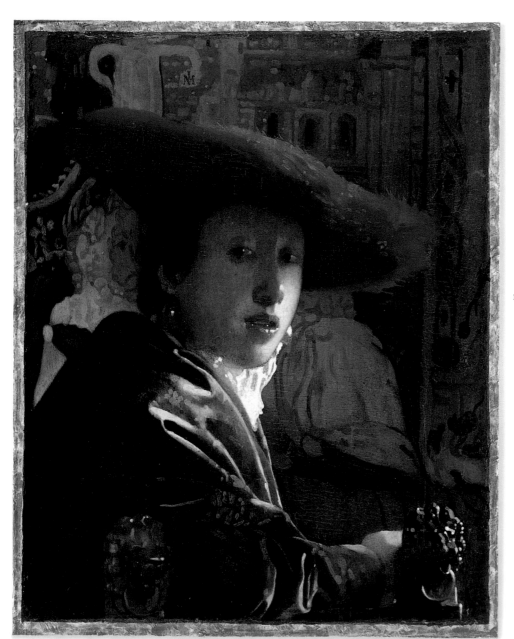

The Girl with the Red Hat

JAN VERMEER *c.1665; 9¼ x 7 in (23.2 x 18.1 cm); oil on panel*
In this small, jewel-like painting, the unfocused, "photographic" nature of the image points to the use of a camera obscura. Vermeer seems to have traced the projected image and then copied the broad pattern of lights and darks directly onto his panel. He then built up the color tones using numerous thin layers of glazes, so that the pigments appear to be suspended in glass. For the hat, he used vermilion of a remarkable intensity, enhanced with red lake.

Lead white reflects the light

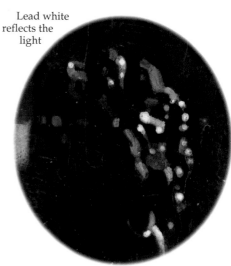

GLOBULES OF LIGHT
In the camera obscura image, small, gleaming highlights on foreground objects melt together and spread into unfocused globules of light. Vermeer has reproduced this effect using thick dots of lead white on the sculpted brass ornaments of the chair, which are in the shape of lions' heads (detail, above).

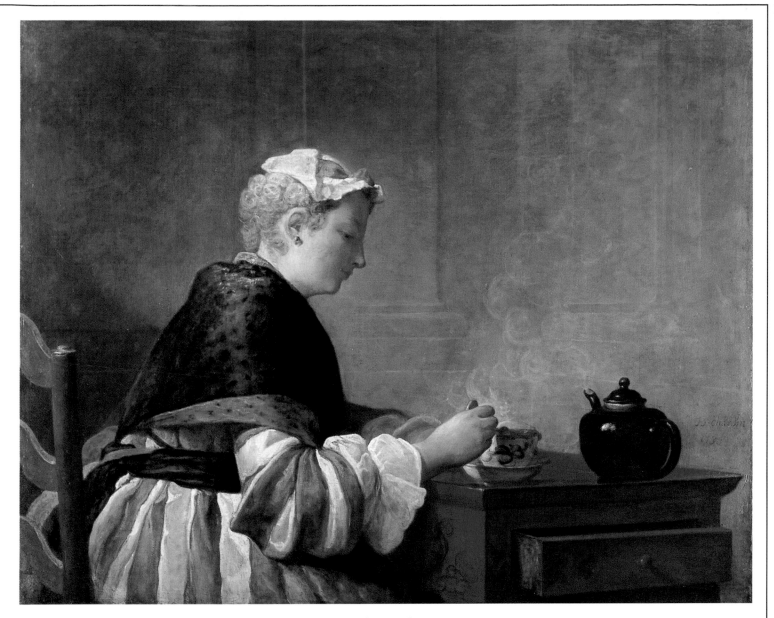

A Lady Taking Tea

JEAN-BAPTISTE CHARDIN *1735; 31½ x 39¾ in (80 x 101 cm); oil on canvas*
Chardin creates different planes of soft light by subtly varying the degree of distinctness and brightness of the objects depicted. The points of highest illumination are the back of the woman's head – her face is veiled in shadow – and the hand in front of the cup. The foremost plane is defined by hue, in the brilliant red of the lacquer cabinet, which seems to advance toward us, just as the blues seem to recede. This is an optical effect: to focus on red (behind the retina), the lens of the eye becomes convex, and, as a result, the color appears larger and nearer. In the case of blue (focused in front of the retina), the lens flattens, and the color appears farther away.

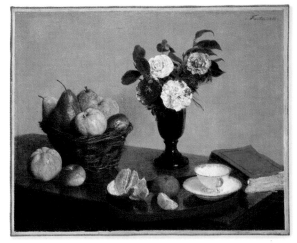

STILL LIFE

Henri Fantin-Latour; 1866; 24½ x 29½ in (62 x 74.8 cm); oil on canvas
Fantin-Latour uses a single source of light to unite objects of a variety of colors and textures: the brittle porcelain, the coarse-skinned fruit, the satin-soft camellias, the basket, vase, and book are all subjected to its modifying effects. There are subtle variations of brightness or intensity, when an object is highlighted or shaded. These are calculated according to its color under normal lighting conditions.

FINE-TUNING COLOR
When a color comes into shadow, Fantin-Latour alters it consistently and proportionately, in a delicate process of color adjustment. The arrangement is disrupted only by the cast shadows (thrown by one object onto another) and the bright reflections (detail, right).

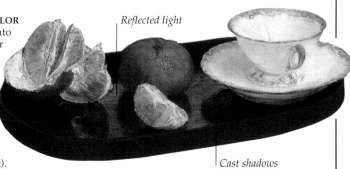

Reflected light

Cast shadows

Rococo decoration

FRENCH ROCOCO STYLE developed in the early 18th century as a reaction to the high-mindedness of classically inspired art. It derives its name from the rock-and-shell work (French: *rocaille*) that decorated garden grottoes. In 1699, the art historian Roger de Piles shocked the French art world by championing color and spontaneity at the expense of "design" – the classical method of composition based on drawing, favored by the establishment. In the debate that followed, de Piles won the day and French artists, like François Boucher (1703–70) and Jean-Honoré Fragonard (1732–1806), set about adapting the majestic colors of Titian and Rubens to the light, amorous atmosphere of society drawing rooms and boudoirs.

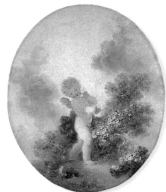

LOVE AS CONQUEROR
Jean-Honoré Fragonard; c.1775; oval: 22 x 18¾ in (55.9 x 46.7 cm); oil on canvas
This decorative oval reflects the playful frivolity of French 18th-century taste. The rosy tints, which caress the flesh, flowers, and clouds, are the enchanted hues of dawn and love.

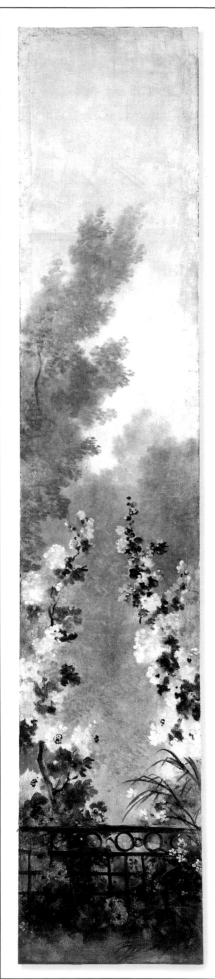

HOLLYHOCKS
Jean-Honoré Fragonard; 1790–91; 125¼ x 25 in (318 x 63.5 cm); oil on canvas
These Chinese-style canvases (left; far right) were painted to decorate the salon at the house of Fragonard's cousin. Their slender grace and airiness is achieved through a vertical type of aerial perspective (p. 24); the eye is swept upward from warm pinks and umbers, through fresh whites and yellows, into clouds of misty foliage.

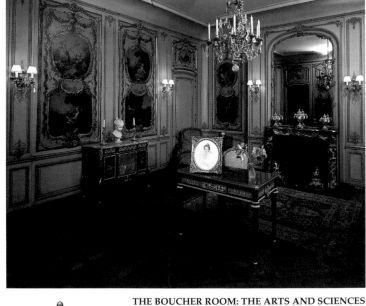

Chinese porcelain covered jar, with "Famille Rose" decoration

Sèvres pot-pourri vase, c.1759

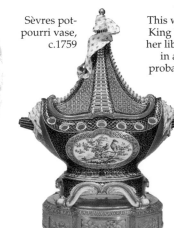

THE BOUCHER ROOM: THE ARTS AND SCIENCES
This whimsical room decoration was commissioned by King Louis XV's mistress, Madame de Pompadour, for her library at the Château of Crêcy, and was completed in about 1750 to 1752. The designs for the panels were probably intended to be used for tapestry chair covers, and the "chocolate box" colors echo the artificial pastel blues, greens, and rosy pinks of Beauvais tapestry shades. Boucher had been producing designs for the Beauvais factory since 1734, and was later to become Inspector of the Gobelins tapestry works (far right).

PORCELAIN BRILLIANCE
The 18th-century craze for everything Chinese also influenced Boucher's coloring. He loved the pinks, sea greens, and turquoise blues of Chinese porcelain (the jar, far left, dates from the Ch'ing Dynasty of 1644–1912). These were imitated in the Sèvres porcelain glazes of his day (left).

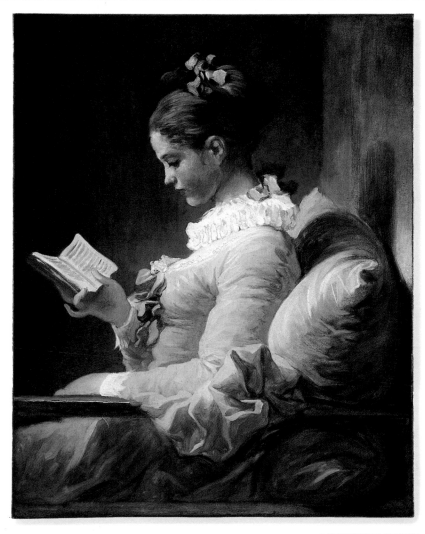

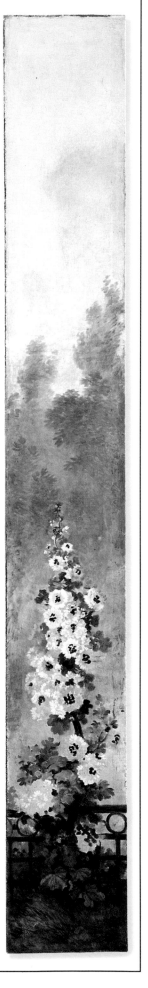

HOLLYHOCKS
Jean-Honoré Fragonard; 125½ x 16½ in (318.8 x 41.6 cm); oil on canvas
The four *Hollyhock* panels were painted to accompany an earlier decorative series, *The Progress of Love.*

A YOUNG GIRL READING
Jean-Honoré Fragonard; c.1776; 32 x 25½ in (81.1 x 64.8 cm); oil on canvas
Aside from his decorative works, Fragonard was famous for the dash and spontaneity of his portraits. He could adapt his palette accordingly, using pale, silken tints for his decorative commissions, and vivid, Rubensian colors for pictures, like this one, in his "rapid manner." Here, the background is sketchily brushed with bitumen brown, so that the figure, in glorious daffodil yellow, seems to bloom before our eyes. The sunlight bounces off the soft lilac cushion, which is so thinly painted that the radiance of the off-white top layer of ground shows through. Its burnt umber shadows add to the overall impression of warmth.

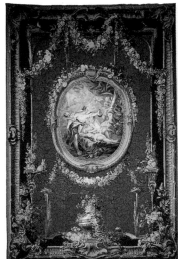

GOBELINS TAPESTRY
Both Boucher and Fragonard produced designs for the highly successful Gobelins tapestry factory in Paris. This involvement carried through to their decorative paintings, where the graceful colors of Gobelins wall hangings and furnishings were often deliberately echoed, so that the whole scheme of the room would harmonize. The influence was two-way: after Boucher's death, Gobelins workers weaved many tapestries based on his paintings, such as this one, after his *Cupid and Psyche.*

Lapis lazuli

"A Tint Book of Historical Colors Suitable for Decorative Work": Gobelins tints

ROCOCO FURNITURE
Fine furniture, like this gilded tripod table with its lapis lazuli top (c.1785), also contributed to an atmosphere of luxury and elegance. The gold was echoed in gilded frames and stucco decoration, while the semiprecious lapis lazuli stone hit a note of pure, unashamed extravagance. Boucher himself collected rare furniture, fragments of lapis lazuli, rock crystals, gems, porcelains, enamel, and mother-of-pearl, reveling in their pretty, sparkling colors.

Gilt bronze

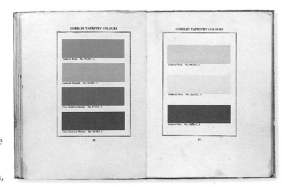

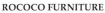

DECORATIVE SHADES
This book of historical tints, used by paint manufacturers to define color combinations, shows some of the famous Gobelins colors. As Inspector, Boucher introduced a wonderful variety of fresh, delicate shades to match the Rococo spirit of design. His paintings were transformed by this interest: he flattened his colors and restricted their range, heightening the transparency of lights and virtually abandoning the rich color of shadow.

Goethe's color theory

In 1810, THE GREAT GERMAN WRITER Johann Wolfgang Goethe (1749–1832) mounted a scathing attack on Newton's "Opticks" in his *"Zur Farbenlehre,"* "The Doctrine of Colors." Goethe opposed Newton's discovery that there were seven colors of the spectrum (p. 6) with his own theory that there were only six, which were seen under natural daylight conditions. To him, color was composed of lightness or darkness: thus yellow was the first color to appear when white was darkened, and blue was the first when black was lightened. Although these ideas were not borne out by physics, Goethe was himself a painter, and his interest in the way we actually see and experience color greatly stimulated later theorists and artists. He observed, for instance, how yellow sunlight produces deep violet shadows, and he described the positive and negative effects of color on the mind.

GOETHE'S DIAGRAMS
The first plate of *"Zur Farbenlehre"* includes Goethe's color wheel (top left) and several diagrams devoted to distorted color perception. The little landscape at the bottom shows how people who cannot perceive blue see the world around them.

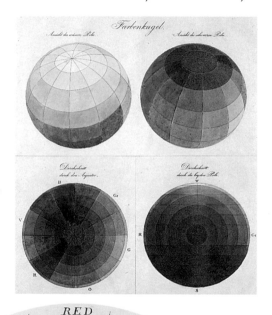

RUNGE'S SPHERE
The German painter Philipp Otto Runge (1777–1810) shared Goethe's interest in the way color could be used in painting. His color sphere (1809), shown here at different angles, establishes a way of measuring pigment color. Color wheels like Goethe's show relationships between hues, but Runge also grades his hues in a scale from light to dark, and saturation to "grayness" (p. 7).

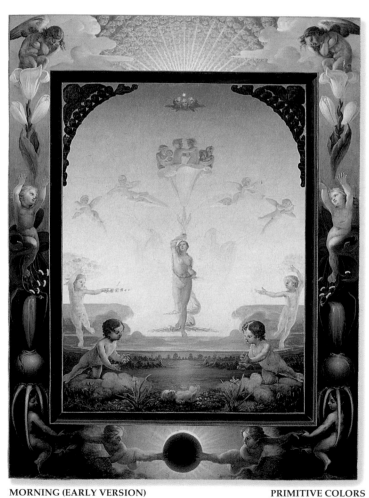

MORNING (EARLY VERSION)
Philipp Otto Runge; 1808; 43 x 33¾ in (109 x 85.5 cm); oil on canvas
Like his contemporary, Goethe, Runge explored the symbolic and spiritual relationships between colors. In *Morning*, these are revealed through the harmonious contrast of golden yellow light and shadowy purple-blue (p. 39). "Color," he wrote, "is the final art, which is, and will always remain, a mystery. It contains the symbol of the Trinity. Light or white is the good, and darkness is the evil ..."

PRIMITIVE COLORS
Before Goethe and Runge, the scientist and naturalist Moses Harris produced a color wheel (c.1770) that emphasized the "primitive" or primary colors – red, yellow, and blue (right). The idea of three primary pigment colors had emerged in the 1720s, but it was not truly accepted by most artists until the mid-19th century.

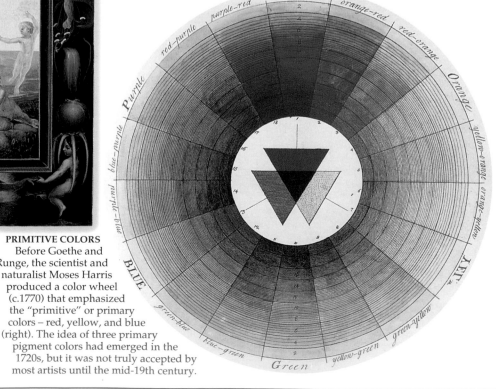

COLORS OF THE SPECTRUM

Goethe's watercolor shows the results of two experiments of light passing through a prism: the colors on the left include the three main colors of Newton's spectrum - orange, green, and violet – which would have been perceived in a dark room from a controlled ray of light; the ones on the right represent Goethe's principal spectral colors – blue, red (which he called *purpur*, meaning "peach blossom"), and yellow – seen by the eye in daylight. With the other colors in this strip – green, blue-red, and yellow-red – these six hues form the basis of Goethe's color circle (below).

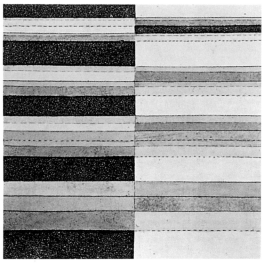

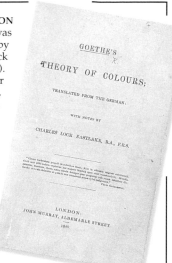

EASTLAKE'S EDITION

In 1840, Goethe's theory was translated into English by the painter Charles Lock Eastlake (title page, right). The great landscape master Turner seized on it, marking his copy with typically bluff notes. What attracted Turner was Goethe's pairing of contrasting colors – which centered on the opposition of yellow and blue – into "positive and negative," "warm and cold," "brightness and darkness," and "light and shadow."

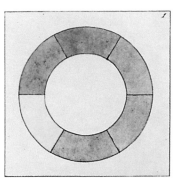

GOETHE'S COLOR CIRCLE

Goethe's wheel was formulated around pairs of colors: yellow and blue; yellow-red (orange) and blue-red (violet); and red and green. For the painter's purposes, red was considered to be as fundamental as his two primaries, yellow and blue. Contrasting colors appear opposite each other: Goethe had observed how green, for instance, produces an after-sensation of red (p. 45).

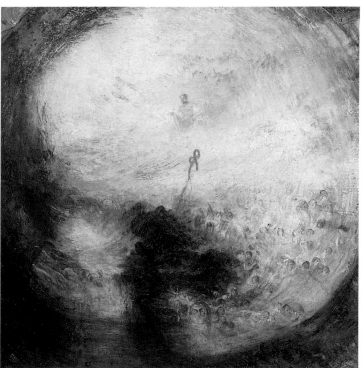

LIGHT AND COLOR (GOETHE'S THEORY) – THE MORNING AFTER THE DELUGE – MOSES WRITING THE BOOK OF GENESIS

J.M.W. Turner; 1843; 30 x 30 in (78.7 x 78.7 cm); oil on canvas

Turner composed a verse to accompany this picture: "Th' returning sun/ Exhaled the earth's humid bubbles, and .../Reflected her lost forms, each in prismatic guise ..." Turner has transformed the entire composition into a bubble, filled with glowing, prismatic hues. Goethe's lively "positive" colors – yellow, red-yellow (orange), and yellow-red – dominate. When Turner was asked what the painting meant, he replied simply, "Red, blue, and yellow."

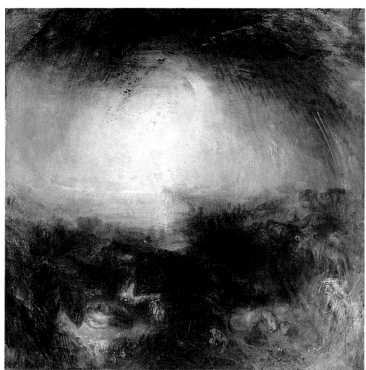

SHADE AND DARKNESS – THE EVENING OF THE DELUGE

J.M.W. Turner; 1843; 30¼ x 30 in (78.7 x 78.1 cm); oil on canvas

In 1843, Turner exhibited a pair of paintings (above; above right), which were influenced by Goethe's theories. The viewer was provided with a vivid and idiosyncratic illustration of Goethe's "positive" and "negative" forces of color, and the conflict between light and shadow. Here, the dark sky and seething waters of the Biblical flood are swept into a whirling mass of blacks and purple blues, surrounding a pool of yellow light in the distance. These colors are placed opposite each other in Goethe's color wheel to show that they complement each other by contrast (pp. 38–39). According to Goethe, yellow and blue symbolize the external forces of God and nature, over which humanity has no control.

THE MATERIALS OF THE ARTIST

Turner was one of the first to distinguish between the artist's materials – painters' pigments (Turner's own box of colors is shown here) – and the material of the physicist – light. Turner realized that when the artist mixed his primary colors, the result was a muddy gray, while the prismatic primaries produce white light (p. 7).

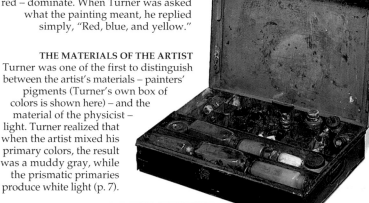

Harmony and contrast

THE LEADING FRENCH Romantic painter Eugène Delacroix (1798–1863) and the chemist Michel Eugène Chevreul (1786–1889) had an immense influence on artistic color practice. Individually, they developed a new idea of color harmony based on contrasts, which was totally opposed to the traditional method of harmonizing and darkening colors with layers of warm-toned varnish. Noticing, like Leonardo and Goethe before them, how harmonies in nature, and in optical science, are achieved through bright contrasts – the green shadows in rosy flesh, for example – they wove together highlights and shadows in webs of complementary colors. The two men arrived at their ideas from differing standpoints: Delacroix from the bravura examples of Veronese and Rubens, combined with his experience of North African light and an admiration for Constable's landscapes; Chevreul from his work supervising the strength and color of dyes at the Gobelins tapestry workshop.

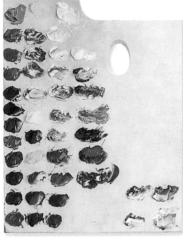

DELACROIX'S PALETTE
Delacroix used this extensive palette of luminous tones for his Saint-Sulpice mural (below). The light material of the palette, as opposed to traditional brown wood (which matched the brownish red grounds of panel paintings), echoes the light ground of the painting and gives a truer sense of how the colors will appear.

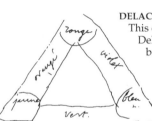

DELACROIX'S COLOR TRIANGLE
This color triangle, from one of Delacroix's North African sketch-books (from his trip there in 1832), highlights the triad of red, yellow, and blue. The mixed, contrasting hues are shown as bridges between them.

THE EXPULSION OF HELIODORUS
Eugène Delacroix; 1856–61; 295¾ x 200 in (751 x 485 cm); oil and encaustic wax
This is one of Delacroix's two huge murals in the church of Saint-Sulpice in Paris, which were greatly admired by the Impressionist painters (pp. 40–41). It exploits a breathtaking variety of color contrasts. Using a dry, thick encaustic wax medium (p. 9), he builds his colors in layers, letting the tints of the underlayers glow through the textured surface. A contemporary writer wrote that Delacroix "interlaces his tones, breaks them up, and, making the brush behave like a scuttle, seeks to produce a tissue whose many colored threads constantly cross and interrupt each other." This analogy to weaving suggests that Chevreul's theories were well known by this time. Delacroix himself was said to have experimented with skeins of different colored wools to produce effects like the mottled green-and-violet flesh tones (below).

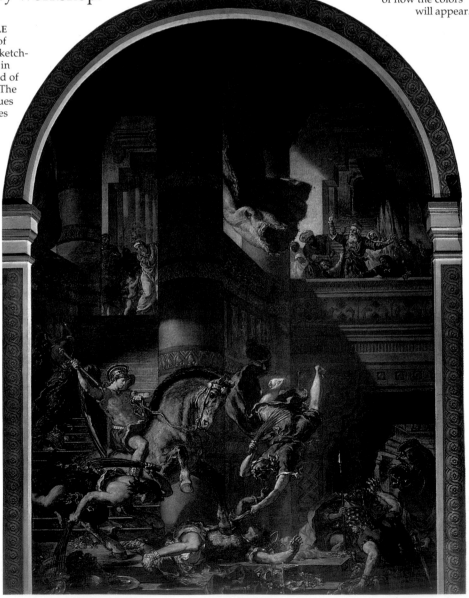

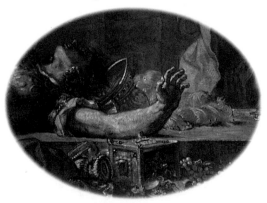

Detail of Heliodorus's arm

Chevreul's law of contrasts

In 1839, Chevreul published his book *On the Harmony and Contrast of Colors*. While working as director of dyeing at the Gobelins works, he had noticed that the brightness of colors did not depend only on the strength of the dyes. Some colors lost their intensity when they were placed next to each other, and from this he developed the simple "law of simultaneous contrast," as to which combinations of color should be avoided, and which arrangements best enhance the purity or forcefulness of hues.

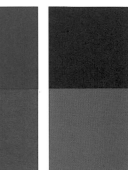

The chemist Michel Eugène Chevreul

CHEVREUL'S COLOR WHEEL
To demonstrate his theories, Chevreul created a color wheel (1861), in which 1,440 dyes are derived from 12 principle colors. It provides a precise system of color measurement, with 20 "degrees" of gradation, from brightness (white at the center) to darkness (at the edges). Complementary colors are shown opposite each other.

COMPLEMENTARY COLORS
Chevreul realized that maximum color contrast could be achieved by placing certain colors side by side. If two colors are placed next to each other, the difference between them appears at its greatest ("simultaneous contrast"), but the effect is most marked when colors are "complementary." He defined the complementary of a hue as the color of the portion of the spectrum it absorbed – for example, red mostly absorbs green. In painter's terms, these complementary pairs are yellow/violet, blue/orange, and red/green (above).

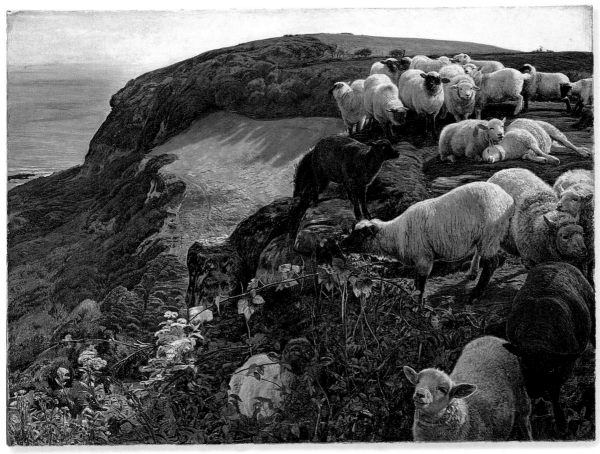

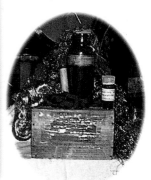

ON ENGLISH COASTS (STRAYED SHEEP)
William Holman Hunt; 1852; 17 x 23 in (43.2 x 58.4 cm); oil on canvas
When this work, by the English Pre-Raphaelite artist William Holman Hunt, was exhibited in Paris in 1856, Delacroix noted, with amazement, "Hunt's sheep." A critic marveled at how "Hunt made a color speak, which, before him, had only slumbered." The sunlit coats of the sheep (detail, right) are tinged with the complementary colors that Goethe had observed in a snowy landscape: "During the day, owing to the yellowish hues of snow, shadows tending to violet have been observable ... as the sun set, and its rays diffused a most beautiful red color ... the shadow color turned to green."

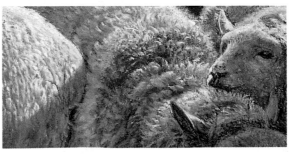

NEW PURPLES
At the time when Holman Hunt and Delacroix were brightening their palettes, vivid new colors were being developed (p. 40). Of these, the most famous was the first synthetic dye, Perkin's mauve (above), made from a distillation of coal tar. It was discovered by an English chemist in 1856.

Impressions of nature

THE IMPRESSIONIST PAINTERS revolutionized color by surrendering themselves to visual experience and mostly working directly from nature. Claude Monet (1840–1926) wrote: "When you go out to paint, try to forget what objects you have before you, a tree, a house, a field, whatever. Merely think: here is a little square of blue, here an oblong of pink, here a streak of yellow, and paint it just as it looks to you ... until it gives your own naïve impression of the scene before you." The attempt to capture nature's "impressions" was never, however, really this naïve. Both Monet and Auguste Renoir (1841–1919) limited their palettes to pure, bright colors, using complementary hues – such as yellow and violet or red and green (p. 39) – to depict the vibration of light and atmosphere. They also used patches or brushstrokes of color to create dazzling, mobile combinations that skillfully evoke fleeting weather conditions and sparkling sunlight.

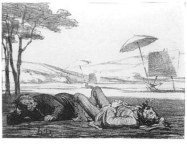

PAINTING IN THE OPEN AIR
The well-known 19th-century caricaturist Honoré Daumier sketched this amusing cartoon of "Landscapists at Work" (1862) – suggesting one of the reasons why painting outdoors was so popular! The Impressionist artists believed that working out in the open air gave their pictures freshness and sincerity.

Chrome yellow

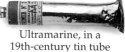

Ultramarine, in a 19th-century tin tube

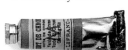

Chrome green, in a 19th-century tin tube

Cadmium yellow

NEW INVENTIONS
The liberation of color was aided by technological innovation. New, vibrant colors came into circulation, based on metallic chromium (c.1815) and cadmium (1820s). Later, the invention of collapsible tin paint tubes (replacing pigs' bladders) made paint much more portable.

RENOIR'S PALETTE
Renoir's handwritten note lists his radiant palette of colors, among them cobalt blue, ultramarine, vermilion, emerald green, chrome yellow, and madder lake (known as "laque de Garance"). The earth tones are few: Renoir comments that "yellow ochre ... and raw sienna are intermediate tones only, and can be omitted, since their equivalents can be made with other colors."

BOATING ON THE SEINE
Auguste Renoir; c.1879; 28 x 36¼ in (71 x 92 cm); oil on canvas
Renoir's brilliant, sunlit painting is a striking example of the Impressionists' use of complementary color. The bright orange rowing skiff glides through a sparkling expanse of pure cobalt blue, each color enhancing the character and intensity of the other. The touches of vermilion, in one of the girl's dresses and in the reflections around the hull, heighten the vibration of the orange further. These effects faithfully record the way the colors actually appear: the eye experiences an after-sensation (p. 45) of orange after gazing at dazzling blue.

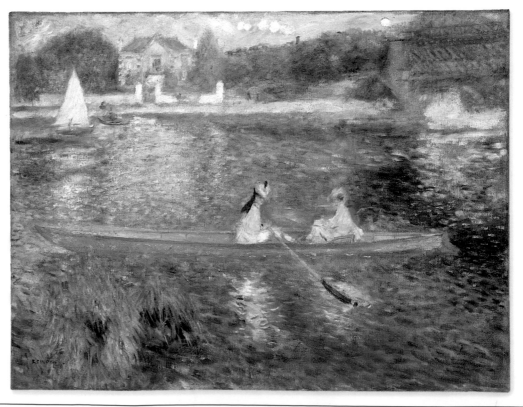

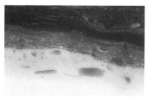

WATER
This cross-section of the water shows dry strokes of pure cobalt blue on top of pale green.

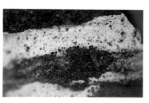

RUSHES
The rushes are painted in viridian, a chromium-based green, worked over chrome yellow.

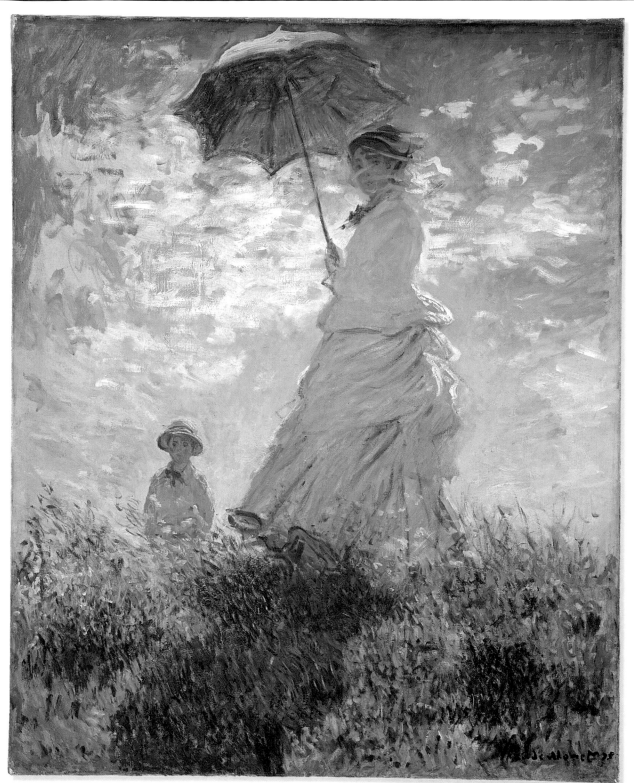

LIGHT AND AIR

Monet's flurries of thick white, painted against the loosely sketched blues of the sky, evocatively describe the way light seems to be tossed on the breeze.

SUNSHINE GROUND

Monet has allowed the creamy ground of the canvas to interact with his color. The violet brings out its complementary hint of yellow, giving the ground a shimmer like soft sunshine.

REDS AND GREENS

Jean's figure is surrounded by a halo of turquoise sky. Its fresh greenish tones set off the red of his hatband and rim, and brighten the glow on his cheeks.

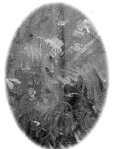

YELLOW HIGH NOTES

The brilliant yellow of the flowers (detail, above) is intensified by complementary blues and violets around the fringes of Camille's dress, providing high notes among the darker, colored shadows.

Woman with a Parasol

CLAUDE MONET *1875; 39½ x 32 in (100 x 81 cm); oil on canvas*
This wonderfully atmospheric painting of Monet's wife Camille and their son, Jean, features the violet-blue shadows that Monet loved. His wife stands on the crest of a hill, silhouetted against the sunlight. Her white dress is suffused with pale violet shadow and swathed in creamy yellow highlights, with little green tints dancing onto it from the grass. "I have at last discovered the true color of the atmosphere," Monet later said. "It is violet. Fresh air is violet."

MONET'S PALETTE
During the 1860s, Monet turned his back on the dark colors that were associated with traditional Old Master techniques, and began to use pure, bright pigments. His palette from this period is dominated by the primary colors, whose importance had been stressed by Delacroix (p. 38), with greens and the indispensable lead white.

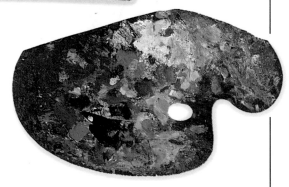

Poetic color

"*To name an object is to suppress three-quarters of the enjoyment ... To suggest it, that is the dream ...* "
Stéphane Mallarmé (1891)

IN THE LATTER HALF of the 19th century, dissatisfaction arose with the naturalistic aims of the Impressionist painters. This led to a revived interest in art as the expression of emotional and decorative ideas, as well as sensual and spiritual experience. In this new climate, the dominant relationship between color and design became the key to the appreciation of the painting. The viewer no longer had to interpret the picture as a faithful record of visual sensations, or look for complex literary meanings. Instead, like poetry, the picture became simply a "suggestion" or an "allusion" – Stéphane Mallarmé, a Symbolist poet, compared a painting by Paul Gauguin (1848–1903) to "a musical poem that dispenses with a libretto [words]." While artists were liberated by the bright palette of the Impressionists, they now emphasized the evocative power of color; Gauguin, for example, used the rhythms of color planes and lines to suggest the heady atmosphere of the Tahitian landscape.

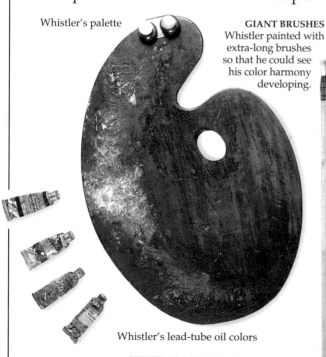

Whistler's palette

GIANT BRUSHES
Whistler painted with extra-long brushes so that he could see his color harmony developing.

Whistler's lead-tube oil colors

WHISTLER'S COLOR ARRANGEMENTS
Whistler's palette was carefully arranged to reflect the harmony of his predetermined color scheme. Each hue was premixed, or adjusted on the canvas – but never mixed on the palette itself. White was placed at the top edge of the palette, with yellow to its left; then came siennas and umbers, blues, and, finally, reds and black. In contrast, Gauguin's palette (far right) shows traditional methods of mixing.

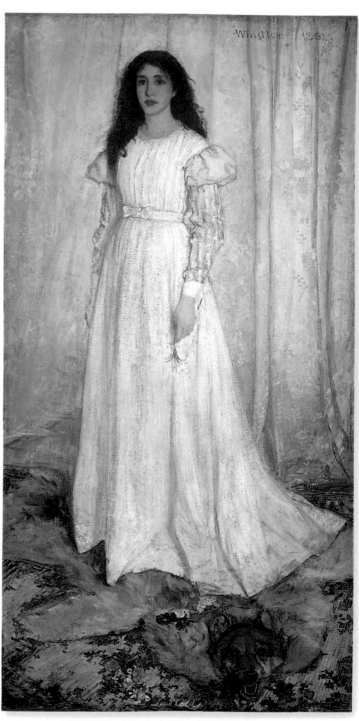

THE WHITE GIRL (SYMPHONY IN WHITE, NO. 1)
James Abbott McNeill Whistler; 1862; 84½ x 42½ in (214.7 x 108 cm); oil on canvas
The Anglo-American painter Whistler (1834–1903) described painting as "the poetry of sight," just as music was the "poetry of sound" (pp. 52–53). He believed that a picture should be appreciated first and foremost as an arrangement or "symphony" of colors and forms, and was exasperated by the public's attempts to discover a hidden literary or symbolic meaning in *The White Girl*. As a result, he emended the original title with "Symphony in White, No. 1." The girl was painted in diffused light, so that her form flattens into broad areas of pale tone and hue. Her features, however, emerge strongly from the mass of dark auburn hair.

LAUS VENERIS
Edward Coley Burne-Jones; c.1873–78;
48 x 72 in (122 x 183 cm); oil on canvas

The Victorian artist Edward Burne-Jones (1833–98) uses rich color to describe the languid and oppressive nature of sensual love. The picture evokes Swinburne's poem of the same title, in which references to blood – "Her little chambers drip with flowerlike red" – suggest love's bitter pleasures.

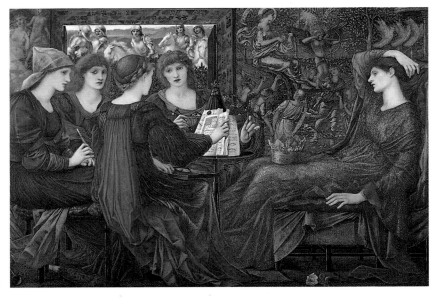

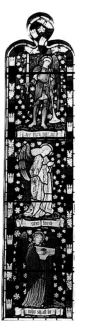
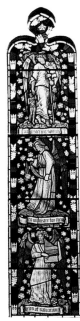

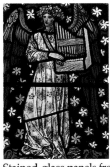

Stained-glass panels from
the Morris Window (left)

STAINED GLASS
Burne-Jones produced outstanding stained-glass designs for the artist William Morris (1834–96), whose famous firm of "fine art workmen" was based on the ideal of medieval craftsmanship. Both used two-dimensional color and light (above) to convey the radiance and simplicity of early Christian piety.

HOLY WOMEN AT THE TOMB
Maurice Denis; 1894; 29¼ x 39½ in
(74 x 100 cm); oil on canvas

The French painter Maurice Denis (1870–1943) believed that "... a picture – before being a war horse or a nude woman or an anecdote – is essentially a flat surface with colors assembled in a certain order." This explains the decorative quality of his work, but the color symbolism is also influenced by Denis's devout religious feeling.

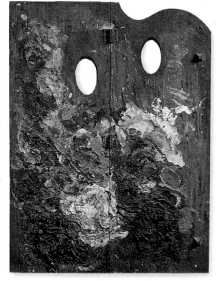

Gauguin's palette

FATATA TE MITI (BY THE SEA)
Paul Gauguin; 1892; 26¾ x 36 in
(67.9 x 91.5 cm); oil on canvas

The Post-Impressionist painter Gauguin was inspired by the pulse and color of life in Tahiti, and the example of Japanese prints (pp. 48–49), to create a vigorously individual ideal of color harmony. He compared his color arrangements to "Oriental chants sung in a shrill voice, to the accompaniment of pulsating notes that intensify them by contrast." In this canvas, for example, he uses flat areas of lavender and mauve-pink for the earth. These unnatural colors are then intensified by the contrasting orange and yellow leaves.

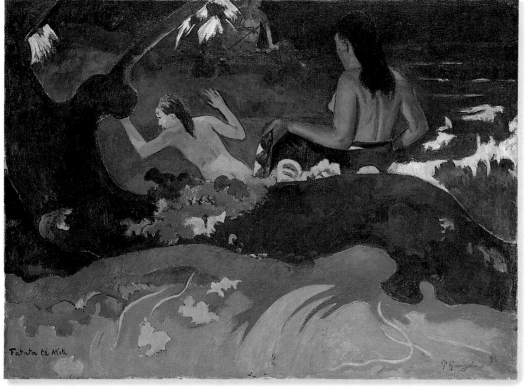

43

Color science

THE FRENCH NEO-IMPRESSIONIST painters Georges Seurat (1859–91) and Paul Signac (1863–1935) were the first to rigorously apply 19th-century scientific color theories to their works. Chevreul's ideas on color contrast (p. 39) were combined with the discovery in the 1850s, by the Scottish physicist James Clerk Maxwell, that colors can be mixed "in the eye," as well as on the palette. Maxwell had demonstrated this using revolving disks, in which, for instance, spinning violet- and green-painted segments produced the optical sensation of blue. In 1879, the American artist and color scientist Ogden Rood proposed that identical optical effects "take place when different colors are placed side by side in lines or dots, and then viewed at such a distance that the blending is more or less accomplished by the eye." This passage had an enormous influence on Seurat, who began to juxtapose dots (French: *points*) of bright color after 1882, systematically creating a technique that became known as *"pointillism"* or *"divisionism."*

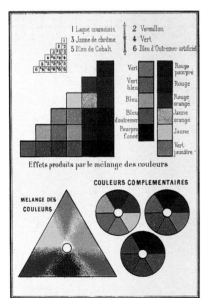

SEURAT'S DOTS
This triple magnification from Seurat's *La Grand Jatte* (below) shows minute dots of color. From a distance, they produce such a small image on the retina (p. 6) that their color does not always register.

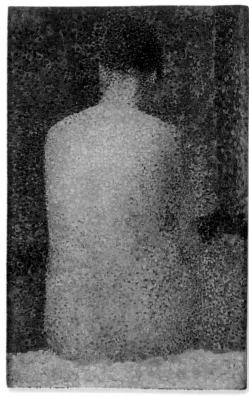

STUDY FOR "LES POSEUSES"
Georges Seurat; 1887; 9¾ x 6¼ in (25 x 16 cm); oil on canvas
This simple study of a nude shows Seurat using dots of contrasting hues. These represent the interweaving of natural flesh colors with the colors of light (yellow and orange), and their complementary tints of shadow (mauve and blue). The lightness of the palette creates a gentle harmony of contrasts.

ROOD'S "COLORS AND APPLICATIONS"
Rood accompanied his detailed discussion of the difference between "optical mixtures" (mixtures in the eye) and paint mixtures with color triangles, tables, and color wheels (1881; frontispiece, left). His proportions of light and color were mathematically measured to prove that optical mixtures could be as luminous as the additive mixture of light (p. 7) – an approach that appealed to the methodical Seurat.

A SUNDAY AFTERNOON ON THE ISLAND OF LA GRANDE JATTE
Georges Seurat; 1884; 81¾ x 121¼ in (207.6 x 308 cm); oil on canvas
Seurat made 23 preparatory drawings and 38 oil studies for this painting alone. There are no earth colors on the surface, just pure tints, which he arranged on his palette in the order of the spectrum. They are used to create a mesh of color, echoing Rood's observation that grass contains "yellowish green, bluish green, reddish, purplish, and brown tints." These hues "flicker and glimmer" close up, but at a distance they tend to appear dull.

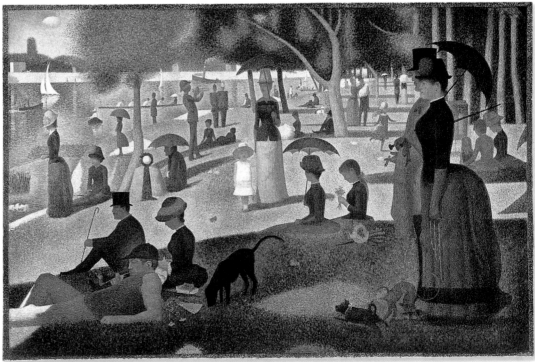

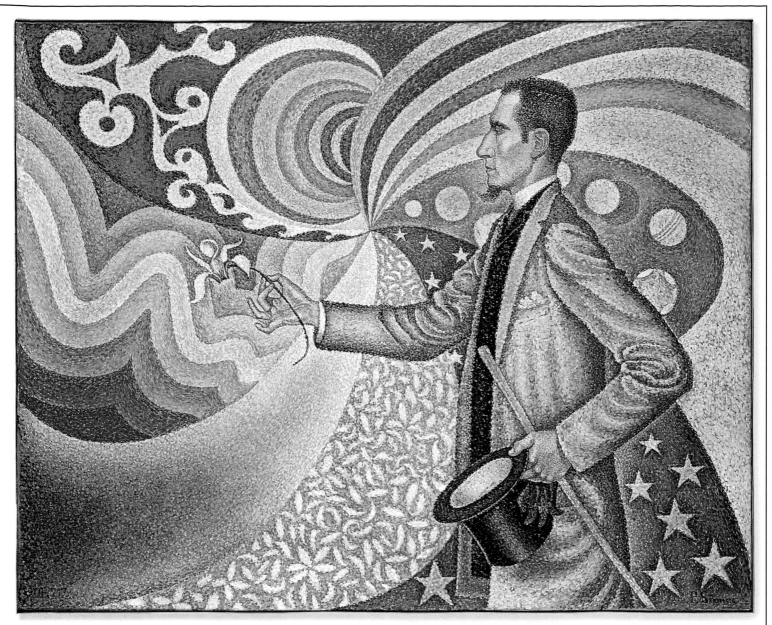

Portrait of Félix Fénéon in 1890

PAUL SIGNAC *1890; 29 x 36¾ in (73.9 x 93.1 cm); oil on enamel*

Here, Félix Fénéon, the critic who championed the art of Seurat and Signac, is flamboyantly depicted against a brilliant kaleidoscope of color and curving line. Signac's portrait is influenced by Charles Henry's publication on the psychological, expressive effects of line and color (right), which Fénéon had greeted as "a flowering mathematical work of art that reanimates all the sciences." These interests are implied in the first part of the title: *Against the Enamel of a Background Rhythmic with Beats and Angles, Tones and Colors ...*

JAPANESE INSPIRATION
The spiraling design in the background of Fénéon's portrait is adapted from a Japanese print that he owned. In one section, Signac has playfully juxtaposed yellow stars in a field of blue (suggesting the American flag) with solar planets in a sky of pink.

THE AFTERIMAGE
This artwork illustrates the "after-image," an illusion described by Chevreul and analyzed by Rood. To experience it for yourself, gaze at the green spade on the left for 15 seconds and then shift your attention to the spot on the right. You will see the spade appear again, but in its complementary color – red (p. 39). The eye will normally avoid this after-sensation by moving continually.

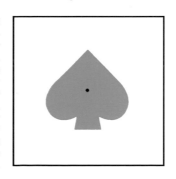

COLOR FROM NEW ANGLES
The scientist Charles Henry believed that warm and cold colors, together with the angle and direction of line, could be used to express "gaiety," "calmness," or "sadness." Artists could use his "Aesthetic Protractor" (above) to put these ideas into practice.

A means of expression

THE DUTCH MASTER Vincent van Gogh (1853–90) and the Norwegian artist Edvard Munch (1863–1944) used color in an exaggerated and distorted way to make powerful personal statements. "Instead of trying to reproduce exactly what I have before my eyes, I use color more arbitrarily, so as to express myself more forcibly," wrote van Gogh. He explained that if he was painting a fair-haired lady, he might choose "orange, chrome, or lemon color" and make "a simple background out of the most intense and richest blue ..." The naturalism of the colors was of no concern to him: what mattered were the strong emotions that the colors aroused. Similarly, Munch used violent color and disturbing linear rhythms to express his particular obsessions. Both men exerted a crucial influence on German Expressionist artists like Ernst Ludwig Kirchner (1880–1938), who jettisoned ideas of conventional color harmony in favor of sharp, clashing colors that "reproduce the pure creative impulse."

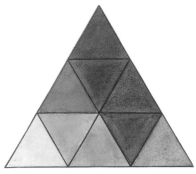

GOETHE'S COLOR TRIANGLE
Goethe had already explored the effects of color on the mind (pp. 36–37). His triangle divides the colors into four "mighty" hues (the four triangles at its apex), the "serene" colors (those in the left angle), and "melancholic" hues (those opposite). He felt their full impact could only be experienced if the eye was "entirely surrounded by one color."

THE COLORS OF "ESSENTIAL" FEELING
The Russian artist Wassily Kandinsky (pp. 52–53) believed that color was the most effective means of communicating feeling. He represented his ideas about the spiritual and emotional power of color in a rotating circle, "like a serpent biting its own tail." Black and white – "the two great possibilities of silence, death and birth" – float outside. The colors within the circle are paired in hot and cold combinations, with yellow, for instance, "the typical earthly color," contrasting with "the heavenly color" blue. "Morbid" violet partners "powerful" orange, while "determined" red is matched with "self-satisfied" green.

> I Yellow
> IV Orange
> III Green
> II White
> II Black
> III Red
> IV Violet
> I Blue

> **"** *I have tried to express the terrible passions of humanity by means of red and green.* **"**
>
> Van Gogh on *The Night Café*

THE NIGHT CAFE
Vincent van Gogh; 1888;
28½ x 36¼ in (72.5 x 92 cm); oil on canvas
In this famous painting, van Gogh has exploited the "clash and contrast of the most alien reds and greens" to express intense human alienation. He had admired the use of these complementary colors (p. 39) in a Delacroix painting, where "blood red" and "terrifying emerald" had been used to dramatic effect. Here, the emerald green ceiling and red walls, lit by the luminous yellow-green lamps, seem to press in on the figures slumped over the tables. Van Gogh also realized that the same hues could be used to express harmony and affection. Love between a couple, he imagined, could be movingly portrayed by the "marriage of two complementary colors" with their "mutual completion" and "vibration."

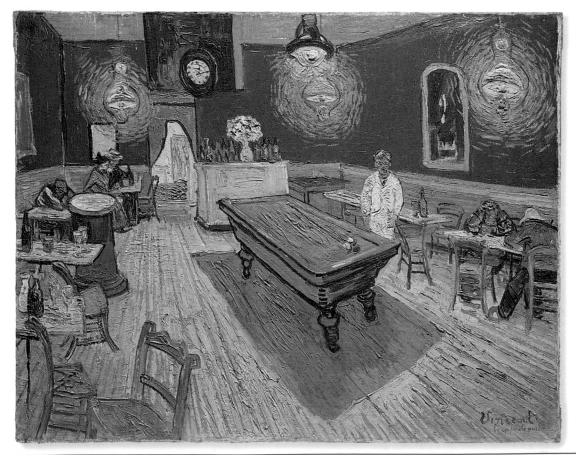

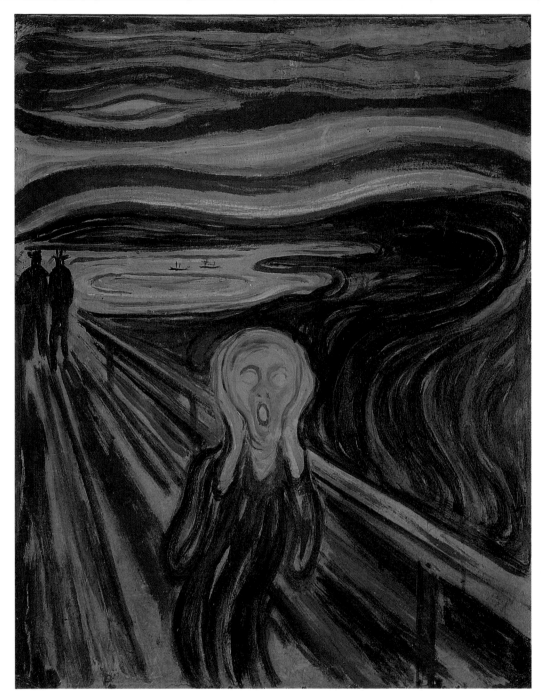

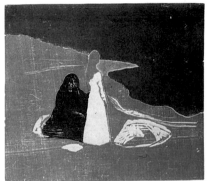

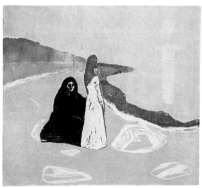

> "*I sensed a scream passing through nature. I painted ... the clouds as actual blood. The color shrieked ...*"
>
> Edvard Munch on *The Scream*

WOMEN ON THE SHORE
In his graphic work, Munch investigated the power that color has over mood and meaning. These two woodcuts are part of a set of six that were printed over a 30-year period. The earliest version (top), made in 1898, shows an old woman and a girl standing on a green shore, against a blue sky. Several color variations later, the final print of the 1920s shows the girl's orange hair intensified to blood red, while the deeper black of the old woman subtly transforms her into a figure of death.

THE SCREAM
Edvard Munch; 1893; 35¾ x 29 in (91 x 73.5 cm); oil, pastel, and casein on cardboard
This jarring image is part of Munch's "Frieze of Life," an extraordinary cycle of paintings based on the subjects of "love and death." The artist explained that *The Scream* was inspired by a walk he was taking along the coastal path at sunset. In his tired and ill state, the clouds appeared to turn to blood red, and all of the colors of nature seemed to shriek. These harrowing effects are conveyed through violent, raw color and swirling linear shock waves. The "scream" seems to rush toward the viewer along the diagonal lines of the distorted perspective, invading the senses through dizzying contrasts of red and mauve. This combination of colors is intended to hurt the eye in the same way as a shrill cry pierces the ear.

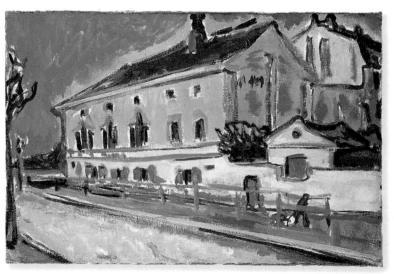

DRESDEN HOUSES
Ernst Ludwig Kirchner; 1909–10; 22 x 35½ in (56 x 90 cm); oil on canvas
Kirchner's discordant colors disobey all of the rules of color harmony. The opposite effect – "clash," where colors react violently with one another – may be less serene, but the acidic color combinations of pink, orange, red, yellow, blue, and green vividly give shape to Kirchner's immediate response to the scene. There is no regard for reality: areas of strident color are bound by outlines in contrasting hues, and the white ground of the canvas is left visible.

Patterns of the East

THE JAPANESE CONTRIBUTIONS to the International Exhibitions, held in London in 1862, and in Paris in 1876, 1878, and 1889, had an enormous impact on Western approaches to color, composition, and design. Artists as diverse as the French Post-Impressionist painters Paul Gauguin and Pierre Bonnard (1867–1947), the Viennese Gustav Klimt (1862–1918), and the American-born James Whistler began to collect Japanese woodcuts and artifacts. They seized on the new potential of pattern that was both decorative and abstract, the asymmetrical arrangements, fascinating color combinations, and the striking balance of fine detail with large ambiguous expanses of color. For van Gogh in particular, the experience of "the brightly colored Japanese prints that one sees everywhere" was overwhelming (the heightened color of 19th-century woodcuts reflect the influence of the West). He began, in his own words, "to see things with an eye more Japanese, [to] feel color differently."

THE JAPANESE COLOR SYSTEM
The classical Japanese color system differed from the West in having five "parent" (primary) colors: red, yellow, blue, black, and white (above). These were mixed to produce nine secondary colors: green, dark blue, sky blue, purple, dark green, orange, brown, and gray. A parent color was rarely used alongside a secondary that was produced from it.

SKETCH FOR "THE BALCONY," NO. 8
James Abbott McNeill Whistler; 1867; 24 x 19 in (61 x 48.2 cm); oil on panel
Whistler based this sketch on two woodcuts by Kiyonaga in his collection, one of which is shown below. The coloring centers on a favored Japanese combination of peachy pinks and turquoise blues, which are woven together throughout the picture. In 1868, Whistler wrote of this to Fantin-Latour, noting that the Japanese "never look for contrast; on the contrary, they're after repetition."

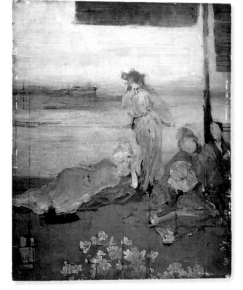

THE FOURTH MONTH
Torii Kiyonaga; c.1790; woodcut
This print by Kiyonaga (1752–1815) employs subtle harmonies of black, white, peach, and warm and cool grays. The watery tones appealed to Whistler; he diluted his paints heavily with gasoline or turpentine to create similar washes of delicate color.

CATCHING FIREFLIES
Eishosai Choki; mid-1790s; woodcut
Eishosai Choki (active 1760s to early 1800s) was admired for his wonderful coloring and startling compositional techniques. Here, a small range of colors is subtly repeated throughout the picture: the orange-red flowers, for instance, are picked up in the ribbons worn by the woman and child, and in the details of their fans. Color is used to create a play of patterns across the surface, from the checks, stars, and floral prints on the kimonos, to the swirls of water and spikes of grass. The print is also dominated by three bands of color: the pale hues of the foreground give way to a solid mass of green, and a large expanse of black (now faded), lit by fireflies.

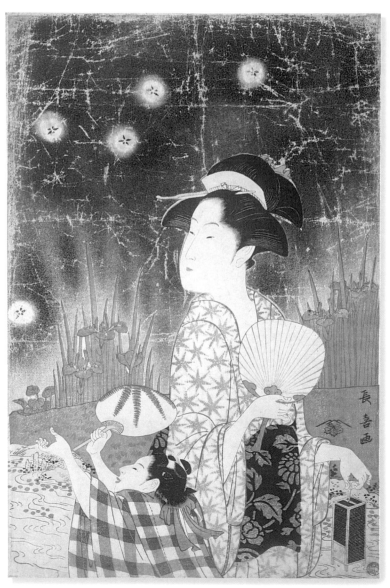

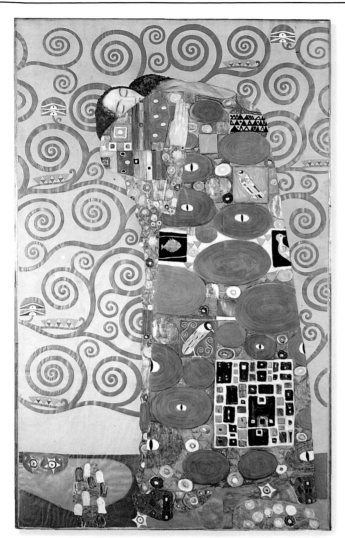

CARTOON FOR THE STOCLET FRIEZE (FULFILLMENT)

Gustav Klimt; 1905–9; 76½ x 47¾ in (194 x 121 cm); appliqué on paper

Klimt collected Japanese kimonos and theatrical Noh costumes (like the one on the right), as well as woodcuts and hanging scrolls. In this working design for the Stoclet frieze, commissioned to decorate the dining room in the house of an industrialist, he swamped his embracing figures in voluptuous robes and locked them within the spiraling patterned background. The irregular areas of gold, black, and silver stand out from the ornamented surface of the man's costume like appliqué patch-work, mingling with a profusion of brightly colored motifs.

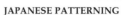

A silk Noh costume, decorated with maple leaves on a checkered blue and gold background

JAPANESE PATTERNING

The exquisite decoration of Noh costumes influenced a number of Western artists. The exotic combination of colors – turquoise with coral, for instance – was inspirational, as in Whistler's sketch (far left). In the asymmetrical patterning, rich, saturated patches of color are scattered amid small, ornamental details.

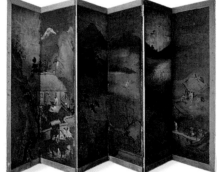

JAPANESE FOLDING SCREEN

In this 18th-century Japanese screen, gold is used to create a floating space that is filled with nondirectional light. Gold was regarded in the East as the only "true" color, because its shimmering surface suggested rather than defined. Such suggestive color areas influenced the move away from realism in the West.

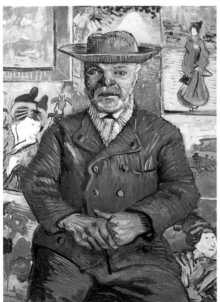

PERE TANGUY

Vincent van Gogh; 1887–88;
25½ x 20 in (65 x 51 cm); oil on canvas

Van Gogh formed a collection of over 400 Japanese woodcuts, buying many from the art dealer and color merchant Père Tanguy. Here, he has set Tanguy against a background of 19th-century colored Japanese prints by his favorite artists, Hiroshige and Kunisada, in a pattern of blacks, reds, yellows, and greens.

In Japanese fashion, Bonnard's brightest colors move across his screen diagonally

STREET SCENE

Pierre Bonnard; 1899; each panel: 56¼ x 18 in (143 x 46 cm); colored lithographs

Bonnard combined the Japanese screen format with graphic techniques, to give his pictures a new type of decorative and spatial dimension. His four-paneled screen is hung with colored lithographs, in which the spareness of detail is balanced against the expansive, "empty" background. The carriages at the top form a unifying band, although they are in the distance: space is suggested by what is known as "vertical" perspective – the higher up on the panel, the farther away an object is.

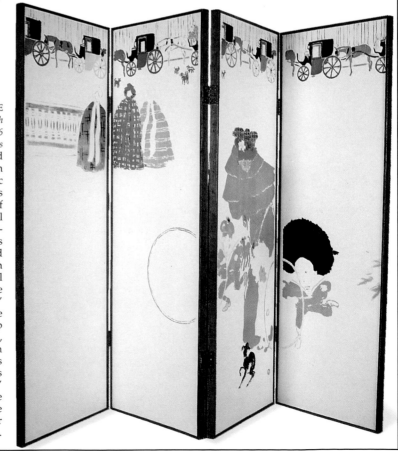

Picasso's changing palette

THE SPANISH GENIUS PABLO PICASSO (1881–1973) devoted his exceptionally long career to exploring endless styles and themes. Color was one of his most versatile tools, ranging from the chilly blues of his Blue Period paintings – so called because of their overall color and the sadness of their mood – to the playful, strident colors of some of his later works. During his Cubist phase, Picasso became preoccupied with line and form (which were traditionally associated with the intellect), and color (linked to the emotions) was virtually eliminated. Subsequently, however, Picasso moved happily between black and white and color, often producing variations on the same theme in a spirit of exuberant experimentation.

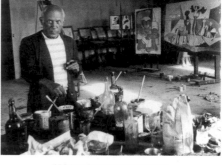

PICASSO IN HIS STUDIO
Picasso surrounded himself with paints, rags, and cans, so that everything was easy to reach. He squatted by his canvas, which was often low down on the easel, mixing his colors by leaning over a table or kneeling on the floor.

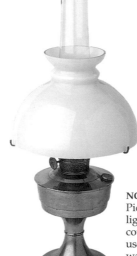

NOCTURNAL LIGHTING
Picasso preferred to paint at night, by the muted light of a lamp. In his early career, he sometimes could not afford the kerosene fuel, which he also used as paint medium: one of his first blue paintings was executed with a paintbrush in one hand and a candle in the other. This weak light made his indigo blues appear even more intense.

THE TRAGEDY
Pablo Picasso; 1903; 41½ x 27¼ in (105.4 x 69 cm); oil on panel
Picasso began "blue" painting in 1901, at the age of 20, as a morbid reaction to a friend's suicide: "I began to paint in blue, when I realized Casagemas had died." The artist was well aware of the color's associations; Symbolist painters in the 1890s had fallen in love with blue's "languid melancholy." In Picasso's own mind, blue was the color of sadness, cold nights, and solitude, and it is no coincidence that his own circumstances were bleak at this time. *The Tragedy*, painted in Barcelona in the winter of 1903, shows a ragged family, barefoot and blue with cold, by the icy blue waters of the sea. Their stark poverty suggests their alienation from society.

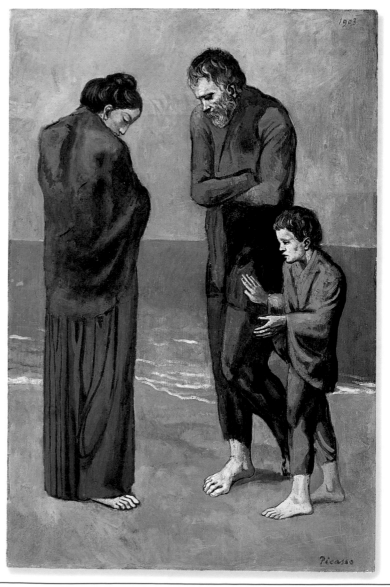

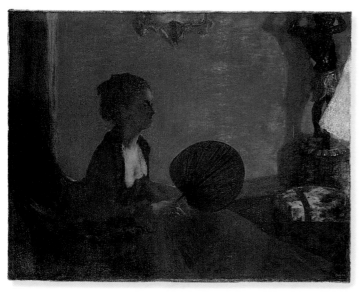

MADAME CAMUS
Edgar Degas; c.1869–70; 28½ x 36¼ in (72.7 x 92.1 cm); oil on canvas
The rich orange-reds of this portrait, by the Impressionist painter Edgar Degas (1834–1917), form a stark contrast to Picasso's cool blues. Here, the color suggests the warmth and comfort of an intimate interior; Degas was fascinated by the effects of artificial light. Picasso was to adopt warmer coloring immediately after his Blue Period, perhaps as a reflection of his happier circumstances, or simply because he was tired of blue. It has been suggested that the tender rose coloring of Picasso's pictures of 1905–7 (the Rose Period) was influenced by his use of the drug opium.

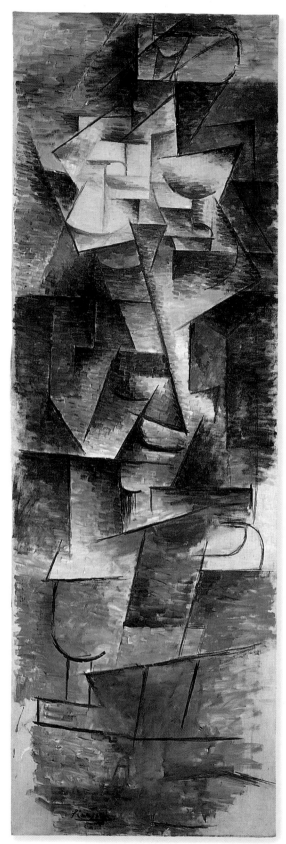

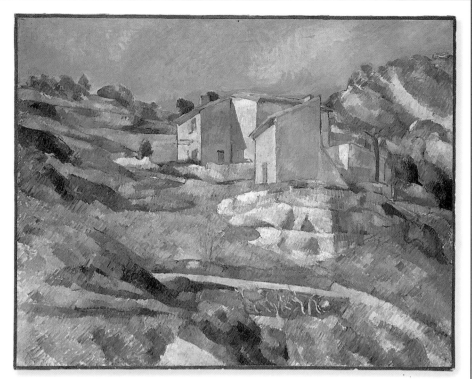

HOUSES IN PROVENCE
Paul Cézanne; c.1880; 25½ x 32 in (65 x 81.3 cm); oil on canvas
Picasso's Cubist paintings draw upon the architectural logic of landscapes by Paul Cézanne (1839–1906). Cézanne set square masses of cool color against warm color, bright color against grayed color, to create light, shade, and, above all, a sense of structure. "Where color has its richness, form has its fullness," he once stated.

LAS MENINAS ("THE MAIDS OF HONOR")
Diego Velázquez; 1656; 125 x 108½ in (318 x 276 cm); oil on canvas
Throughout his career, Picasso was drawn to the color harmonies of his great Spanish predecessor, Diego Velázquez (1599–1660). When a friend commented on the "Spanishness" of Picasso's tans, blacks, browns, and whites, which characterize his Cubist paintings and his studio interiors of the 1950s, Picasso replied, "Velázquez." He based a series of paintings directly on *Las Meninas* (below).

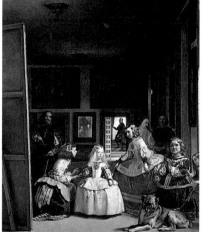

LAS MENINAS: THE INFANTA MARGUERITA MARIA, NO. 27
Pablo Picasso; September 14, 1957; 39½ x 32 in (100 x 81 cm); oil on canvas
The Infanta is based on the little Spanish princess at the center of Velázquez's *Las Meninas* (above). Picasso had set up a huge enlarged black-and-white photograph of Velázquez's picture in his studio in 1957, and then devoted most of the next five months to painting 44 variations on it, dating each picture precisely. Some of his pictures include the whole composition, in shades of black and white, while others pull it apart, and color it with extraordinary inventiveness. Here, Picasso has depicted the Infanta turned toward us so that most of her face is in dark green and violet-blue shadow. Picasso may have been aware that if neutral colors, such as those in *Las Meninas* (above), are stared at, afterimages of their complementary appear (p. 45), producing an illusion of color.

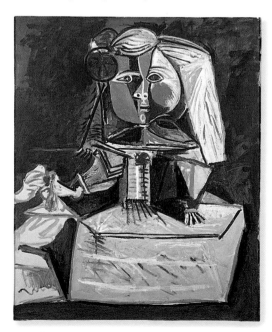

NUDE WOMAN
Pablo Picasso; 1910; 73¾ x 24 in (187.3 x 61 cm); oil on linen
This work is a key painting of the brief phase (to 1912) known as "Analytical" Cubism. In this style developed by Picasso and Georges Braque, space and forms were analyzed, disintegrated, and reassembled until they were almost unrecognizable, while colors were remorselessly reduced to black, white, brown, and gray. These are the colors of spatial planes, voids, and edges, where darkness is contrasted with brightness to suggest fragmented forms.

Color and music

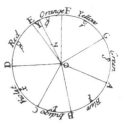

A MUSICAL COLOR WHEEL
Newton formed his seven colors of the spectrum (p. 6) into a color circle, matching each rainbow hue to a portion of the musical scale.

THE LINK BETWEEN COLOR AND MUSIC, the "sensations" of the eye and the ear, reached a new significance in 20th-century art. "Color," wrote the Russian artist Wassily Kandinsky (1866–1944), "is the keyboard, the eyes are the harmonies, the soul is the piano with many strings. The artist is the hand that plays, touching one key or another, to cause vibrations in the soul." This notion of musical and color harmony stretches back across the centuries. The artist known as the Master of the Saint Lucy Legend used the beauty of shot color to suggest the divine harmonies of 15th-century choral music, while the Renaissance Italians equated musical measures with mathematical balance and proportion. However, in the 20th century, artists like Paul Klee (pp. 54–55) and Kandinsky used color in a highly theoretical and philosophical way – associating tone with timbre (the sound's character), hue with pitch (whether a sound is pitched high or low), and saturation with the volume of sound. Kandinsky even claimed that when he saw color, he heard music: he spoke of the azure flute, the blue cello, and the bass echo of black.

MUSICAL VIBRATIONS
In the 17th and 18th centuries, the colored wavelengths of light (p. 6) were thought to behave like the trembling vibrations of sound in a bell or the string of a lute. Artists imitated these by using ringing color combinations.

MARY, QUEEN OF HEAVEN
Master of the Saint Lucy Legend; c.1485/1500; 78½ x 63¾ in (199.2 x 161.8 cm); oil on panel
In this panel, by the Flemish Master of the Saint Lucy Legend, the Assumption and Coronation of the Virgin (where Mary is raised up to Heaven and crowned) is accompanied by the glorious music of singing and playing angels. The spiritual harmony of their music is expressed through radiant chords of color, which are carefully distributed among the angels' robes. Leonardo compared the harmonious proportions of painting to "many different voices joined together and singing simultaneously ... which gives such satisfaction to the sense of hearing that listeners remain spellbound with admiration, as if half alive." At the time this altarpiece was painted, music was mainly sung, with instruments such as the lute, viol, and harp being used to multiply the vocal parts.

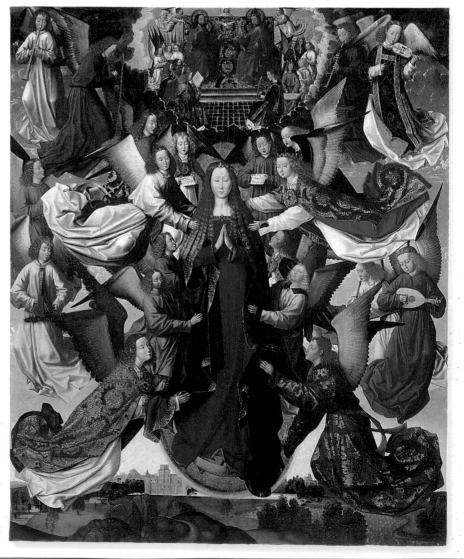

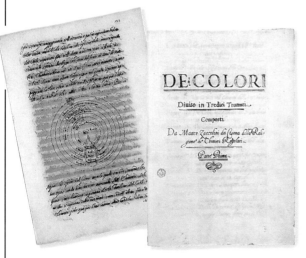

ZACCOLINI'S COLOR MUSIC
In *"De Colori"* (Italian: "About Color"), which was popular in 17th-century Roman artistic circles, Matteo Zaccolini created a type of color-music to be used therapeutically – as in the tarantella dance. The tarantella rhythms were thought to cure the poisonous bite of the tarantula, and Zaccolini believed that colors, matched to the musical chords, could aid the process.

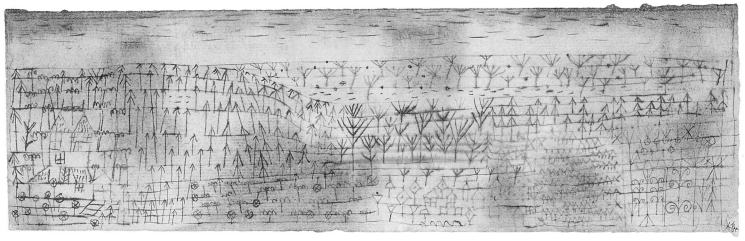

JUNGER WALD (YOUNG FOREST)

Paul Klee; 1925; 3¾ x 12¾ in (9.8 x 32.2 cm); pen and ink, and watercolor on paper, mounted on cardboard
Klee came from an exceptionally musical family and was himself a very gifted violinist. He often incorporated musical theory into his pictures, using expressive color and meticulous linear forms to create a harmonious synthesis of color and line. Here, tiny arrows, bird's claws, and other suggestive shapes are the symbols of young trees and thickets, but they are arranged in horizontal bands as if they were hundreds of notes sitting on a musical stave. The fine pen lines mark out the musical rhythms and measures, and the hazy areas of color are almost like the parts played by different instruments in an orchestra, which enhance the richness of sound. Klee's fresh tints of rose, yellow, green, and blue also suggest growth and renewal.

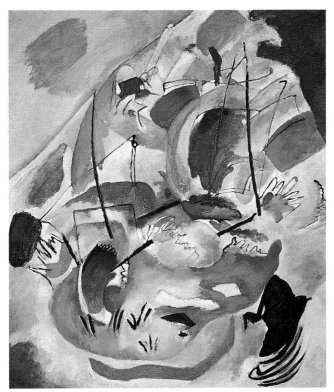

IMPROVISATION 31 (SEA BATTLE)

Wassily Kandinsky; 1913; 55½ x 47¼ in (140.7 x 119.7 cm); oil on linen
Kandinsky described his "improvisations" as "unconscious expressions of an inner impulse." Here, two battling sailing ships are just recognizable, but the painting is more concerned with Kandinsky's response to the idea of conflict. He has used color – trumpeting yellows, loud and restless reds and oranges – to suggest the noise of battle, and isolated greens and blues to show the disruption of harmony.

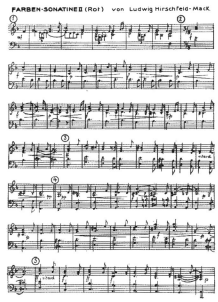

Ludwig Hirschfeld-Mack:
Color sonatina in red

MUSIC IN THE KEY OF "RED"

The Bauhaus, a German school of craft and design, believed in bringing the arts together. Both Klee and Kandinsky taught there. This "Color Sonatina in Red" was composed by one of its artists, Ludwig Hirschfeld-Mack, to accompany his colored light compositions.

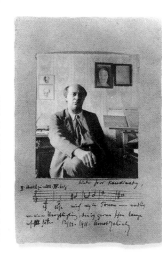

THE COMPOSER SCHÖNBERG

Many of Kandinsky's musical ideas were inspired by his close friendship with the composer Arnold Schönberg, who had broken away from traditional rules of musical composition. This photo of Schönberg, dated December 12, 1911, bears a cryptic message: "Dear Mr. Kandinsky, I free myself in notes from an obligation that I would have liked to fulfill long ago."

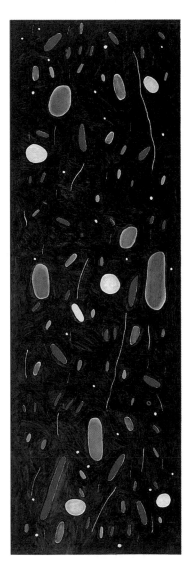

THE SONG OF THE VOWELS

Joan Miró; 1966; 144 x 45¼ in (366 x 114.8 cm); oil on canvas
The Catalan artist Joan Miró (1893–1983) sought an abstract equivalent to musical ideas, using disks of color. The song of the title refers to a poem, "Vowels," by the French poet Rimbaud, in which colors are matched to vowels (A to black, E to white, I to red, O to blue, and U to green). Miró has varied the color intensity, shape, and size of each disk, so that they seem to range from a full musical note to a tiny rhythmic accent.

Oriental light

IN APRIL 1914, THE SWISS ARTIST Paul Klee (1879–1940) set out for Tunisia in North Africa with two painter friends, Auguste Macke (1887–1914) and Louis Moilliet. They went in the hope that, like Delacroix, Monet, Renoir, and Matisse before them, their art would be transformed by the revelation of Oriental color and light. Previously, Klee had worked mostly in black, white, and tonal grays, but as soon as he arrived he brought out his bright pans of watercolor. The pictures he painted in Tunisia, and in the years just after his return, are filled with delicate yellows, blues, mauves, greens, and the luminous white of the watercolor paper; later he used much more intense colors to conjure up the sun-flooded Tunisia of his memory. By the time he had reached his final destination, the ancient Arabic city of Kairouan, Klee had come to this euphoric realization: "Color possesses me. I no longer have to pursue it. It will possess me always. I know it. This is the meaning of this happy hour: color and I are one. I am a painter."

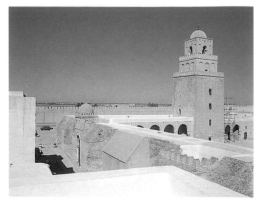

THE CITY OF LIGHT
On April 15, Klee and his companions arrived at Kairouan, the "city of a hundred mosques." Their three-day stay had a profound effect on Klee. Here, he saw the color theories of his Parisian friend Robert Delaunay (p. 7) come to life: the architecture was shaped by pure color and light, and the contrasting hues of sunlight and blue- and violet-tinged shadow vibrated with vitality.

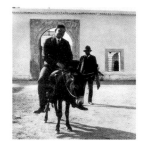

OUTSIDE THE GATES OF PARADISE
This photo shows Klee and Macke (on the donkey) in 1914, outside the walls of Kairouan. The city was described in their 1911 Baedecker guide as one of the four gates to Paradise.

AFRICAN INTRICACY
The intricate patterns and colors of the Near East influenced Klee, just as they had Matisse (p. 57). This Moroccan textile, owned by Matisse, echoes the delicate latticework of the window grates in Morocco and Tunis. Klee often superimposed this patterning on his colors to give them a sense of rhythm (p. 53).

KAIROUAN I
Auguste Macke; 1914; 8½ x 10½ in (21.4 x 27 cm); watercolor on paper
Macke's watercolor of Kairouan at night explores the relationships between light and darkness, and warm and cool color, which fascinated both him and Klee. The blue, cool colors divide the sky into strips, and the sands into patches of green, blue, and violet shadow; the warm colors, tending toward yellow, describe the glowing forms of the architecture and the heat that still radiates from the sands. Klee enthusiastically described their experience of an evening there as: "The essence of *A Thousand and One Nights*, which is, however, 99 percent real. What an aroma, how penetrating, how intoxicating, and, at the same time, simple and clear."

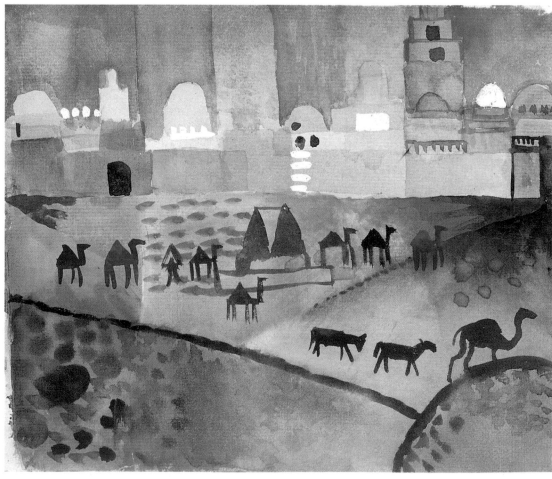

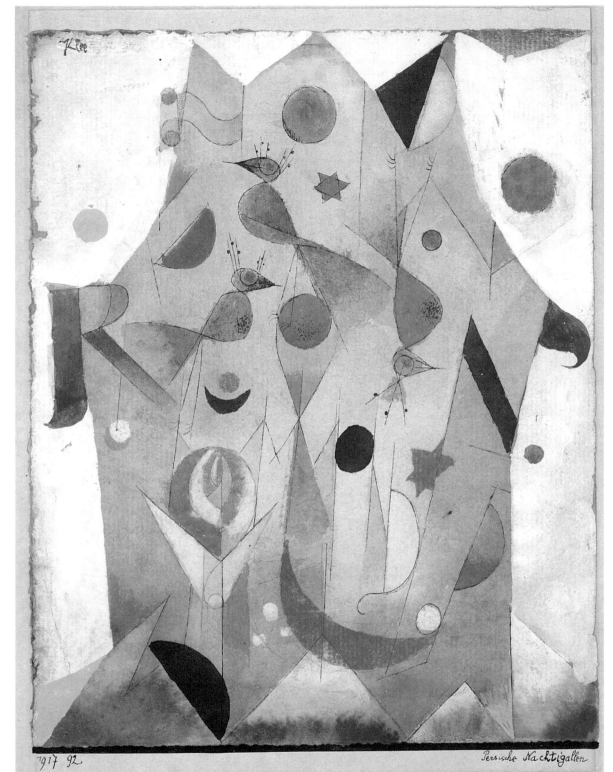

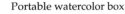

1917 92   Persische Nachtigallen

Persian Nightingales

PAUL KLEE *1917;*
9 x 7¼ in (22.8 x 18.1 cm);
gouache, watercolor, pen,
ink, over graphite on paper

This poetic picture
was painted during
the First World War,
while Klee was in
military service. His
friends Macke and
Franz Marc had been
killed in action, and
Klee spent much of his
time in meditation.
This watercolor
combines the effect of
his trip to Tunis with
the influence of the
classic Chinese poems
in which he immersed
himself. The delicate
washes of color are
united with fine-line
Arabic letters (R and
N), interlaced with
birds, moons, and
stars. The colors are
a "blond" echo of the
"southern moonrise"
of Kairouan that
had so inflamed
Klee's soul.

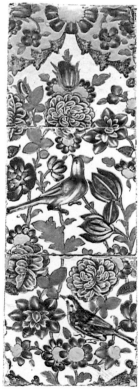

WATERCOLOR MEDIUM
The watercolor medium
is perfect for capturing the
radiance of light. Pigment
is bound with a water-
soluble medium, usually
gum arabic from the
acacia tree, and lighter
tones are obtained by
thinning with water. The
watery glazes of color are
so translucent that the light
from the paper shines through.

Portable watercolor box

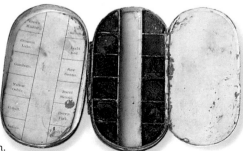

THE UNIVERSE IN MINIATURE
Klee's combination of birds and
blossoms resembles the designs of
Persian tiles (right) and illuminations.
He loved the hypnotic miniature patterns
of these arts, because their natural detail
evoked a whole "other" world of reality;
a friend noted that Klee saw infinity in
a green leaf or a butterfly wing. In
the delicate color balances, Klee also
found confirmation of Cézanne's idea
that color is "the place where our
spirits and the universe meet."

Matisse's pure color

"WHEN I PAINT GREEN, it doesn't mean grass; when I paint blue, it doesn't mean sky." In this way, the 20th-century master Henri Matisse (1869–1954) summed up the essence of his approach to color. From the brilliant vigor of his early Fauvist paintings to the luminous serenity of his later masterpieces, Matisse freed color once and for all from its literal, descriptive role – his choice of shades was governed by "observation," "feeling," and "the very nature of each experience." In order to match his colors to the intensity of his emotions, Matisse deliberately organized them in the most expressive way. If he needed a balance of pure, unmixed hues to provide a restful surface for the eye, he did not hesitate to create it. Often, he would change his colors while in the process of painting, until he achieved the harmonious combination of tones that he could already "see" in his mind's eye.

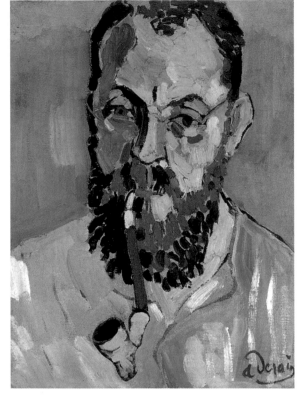

HENRI MATISSE
André Derain; 1905; 181 x 137½ in (46 x 34.9 cm); oil on canvas
Derain painted this portrait of Matisse when they were both members of the "Fauves" (French: "wild beasts"). A critic had coined this unflattering name in response to the savage energy and fierce, unnaturalistic color of their pictures. (Matisse also wore a furry overcoat at the group's first exhibition!) The Fauves used vigorous daubs of paint, wielding colors like "sticks of dynamite." "We were always intoxicated with color, with words that speak of color, and with the sun that makes colors live," wrote Derain.

AFRICAN INSPIRATION
Matisse was among the first French artists to realize the power of African art. His fellow painters André Derain (1880–1954) and Maurice de Vlaminck, stimulated by their visits to the primitive exhibits in the Paris Trocadéro, had begun to collect African masks and statuettes, and Matisse soon followed suit. (It was Matisse who introduced Picasso to African art.) The pure impulses of these artifacts inspired them to approach nature with the same directness and lack of prejudice.

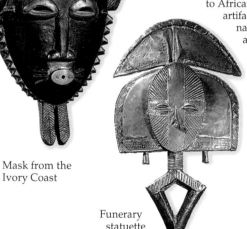

Mask from the
Ivory Coast

Funerary
statuette
from Gabon

HARMONY IN RED
Henri Matisse; 1908–9; 71 x 86½ in (180 x 220 cm); oil on canvas
Here, Matisse has used color of equal brightness and saturation throughout the picture, so that no area is seen to be the background. The figure, the table, the wall, the window, the lemons – all engage our attention equally, inviting our eye to move over the vibrating surface. The mutual attraction of these intense colors is similar to that of the Persian miniatures loved by Matisse (p. 27). But the huge expanse of red – with the red table flattening out to become unified with the red wall – flouts the rules of decorative harmony, in which bright patches of color were usually small. He originally painted *Harmony in Red* in blue or blue-green, later altering the color to create "a cocoon of warmth."

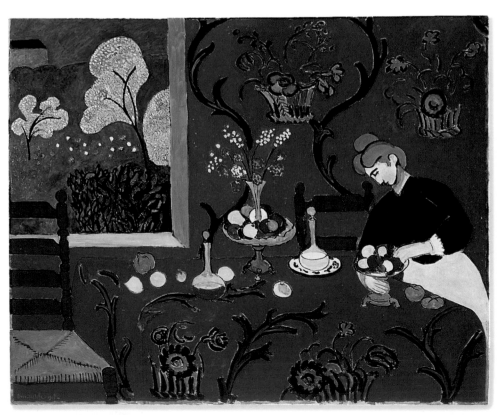

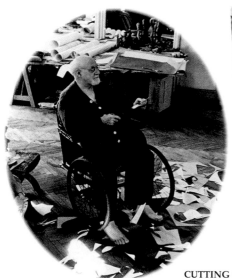

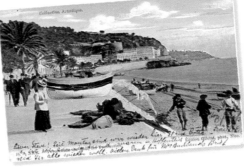

THE LIGHT OF THE RIVIERA

From 1917, Matisse spent a great deal of his time in Nice on the French Riviera, making his home there in 1921. "When I realized that I would see that light every morning," he wrote, "I could not believe in my own happiness." Matisse's idol, Cézanne, had also lived and worked in this wonderful southern Mediterranean light: "The sunlight here is so intense," Cézanne noted, "that it seems to me that objects are silhouetted not only in black and white, but also in blue, red, brown, and violet ... This seems to me to be the opposite of modeling."

CUTTING INTO COLOR

Following two operations for duodenal cancer in 1941, Matisse was confined to a wheelchair. Undaunted by the fact that he could no longer paint at an easel, he began to make pictures out of pieces of cut-up colored paper that had first been painted in gouache (the texture of the paint is clearly visible; right). "Cutting directly into color," he wrote, "reminds me of the direct action of the sculptor carving stone." At last, he had found a form in which line (drawn by his scissors), color, and idea could be realized simultaneously.

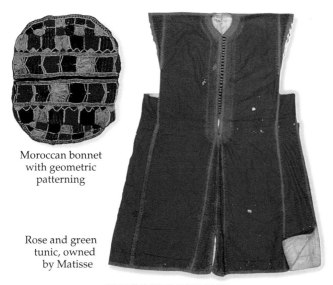

Moroccan bonnet with geometric patterning

Rose and green tunic, owned by Matisse

OBJECTS FROM THE EAST

Throughout his life, Matisse drew inspiration from Oriental cultures. He traveled to Algeria, Russia, Tangiers, and Polynesia, bringing back textiles (p. 54), costumes, and even seaweed and flowers. This Moroccan bonnet and tunic are two of the many beautiful items he surrounded himself with. From these – along with Persian miniatures, Russian icons, Islamic rugs, ceramics, and primitive sculptures – he learned about new color harmonies and the rhythms of line.

BEASTS OF THE SEA

Henri Matisse; 1950; 116¼ x 60½ in (295.5 x 154 cm); paper collage on canvas

This eight-foot-high (three-meter) canvas, filled with spiraling cut-out forms, recalls the artist's trip to Polynesia of 20 years earlier. It is based on Matisse's account of a "grayish jade green lagoon" with pastel-tinted coral branches, "around which pass shoals of small fish, blue, yellow, and striped with brown ... And dotted about everywhere the dark brown of the sea cucumbers ..." His feelings for this watery paradise are re-created in clashing harmonies of mint, apple, and grayish greens, pinks, purples, and mustard and lemon yellows. Recognizable shapes are stacked in blocks of color, interlacing "like a cord or a serpent," as Matisse intended.

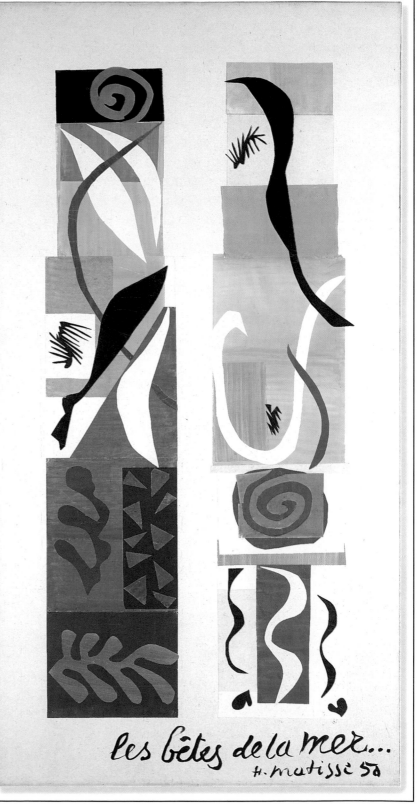

les bêtes de la mer...
H. matisse 50

Abstract power

ABSTRACT ART – in which there are no recognizable references to the outside world – relies heavily on the dynamic nature of color. By the early 20th century, photography had destroyed the documentary value of the realistic painted image, and artists were becoming increasingly interested in deepening and universalizing their sensations and ideas. For many, this meant a return to basics: the Dutch painter Piet Mondrian (1872–1944) used the relationships between lines and colors to bring into play "the whole sensual and intellectual register of the inner life." His cool, geometric abstraction contrasts with Kandinsky's expressive "improvisations" (p. 53). The emotive power of color was realized most intensely in the all-enveloping canvases of the Russian-American artist Mark Rothko (1903–70), in which color overwhelms the senses.

> *"We all pay homage to clarity."*
>
> Piet Mondrian, from his essay "Plastic Art and Pure Plastic Art" (1945)

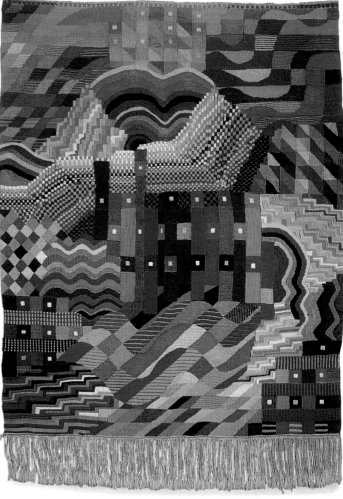

WALL HANGING IN RED AND GREEN
Gunta Stölz; 1926–27; 76¾ x 44½ in (195 x 113 cm); warp linen and weft cotton
In the 1920s, Gunta Stölz (1897–1983) ran the weaving workshop at the influential Bauhaus school of design. This stunning wall tapestry closely reflects the teachings on color of the Swiss painter and designer Johannes Itten, whose Bauhaus classes she attended. Itten believed that color and form were inseparable – "Form and color are one" – and that the simplest, most expressive elements were geometric shapes and the colors of the spectrum. He advised artists to exploit different kinds of color contrasts, and to be sensitive to the emotional affinities between certain colors and certain shapes.

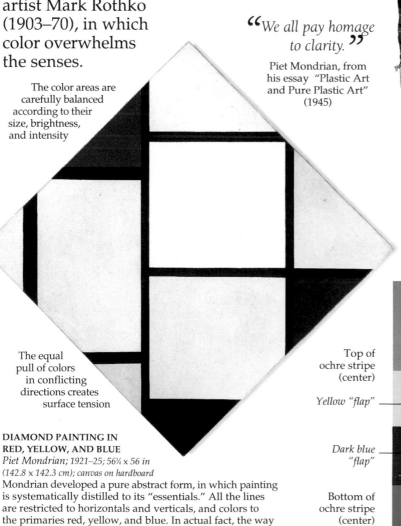

The color areas are carefully balanced according to their size, brightness, and intensity

The equal pull of colors in conflicting directions creates surface tension

DIAMOND PAINTING IN RED, YELLOW, AND BLUE
Piet Mondrian; 1921–25; 56¼ x 56 in (142.8 x 142.3 cm); canvas on hardboard
Mondrian developed a pure abstract form, in which painting is systematically distilled to its "essentials." All the lines are restricted to horizontals and verticals, and colors to the primaries red, yellow, and blue. In actual fact, the way these elements interact is far more complex. Here, the square picture is presented in diamond format, which introduces the diagonal lines of the edges of the board. And in addition to the primaries, white, black, and gray set up new color tensions.

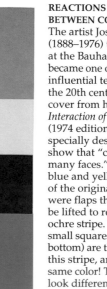

Top of ochre stripe (center)

Yellow "flap"

Dark blue "flap"

Bottom of ochre stripe (center)

REACTIONS BETWEEN COLORS
The artist Josef Albers (1888–1976) taught at the Bauhaus and became one of the most influential teachers of the 20th century. This cover from his book *Interaction of Color* (1974 edition) was specially designed to show that "color has many faces." The dark blue and yellow strips of the original artwork were flaps that could be lifted to reveal an ochre stripe. The two small squares (top and bottom) are the tips of this stripe, and are the same color! They only look different due to the surrounding hues.

Red, Black, White on Yellow

MARK ROTHKO *1955; 105 x 93 in (266.7 x 236.2 cm); oil on canvas*

Rothko developed a severe and distinctive style, in which imposing canvases pulsated with large areas of color. His pictures are often hung together in one room, so that the setting is filled with their mysterious resonance. "By saturating the room with the feeling of the work," Rothko wrote in 1954, "the walls are defeated, and the poignancy of each single work [is] more visible." The works are hung low, without frames, to ensure that the viewer experiences the drama of color directly.

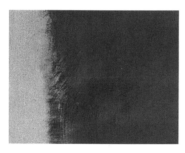

ENIGMATIC VAGUENESS
Rothko used his color almost like a stain. It seeps beyond its blurred "edges," as in this detail, and seems to hover above the picture surface. The thin, brown ground of the canvas glows through the tones, giving them a strange, lurid quality. Unhappily, Rothko often used experimental materials and impermanent organic colors (p. 62). Now, many of his paintings are literally fading away.

IKB 79
Yves Klein; 1959; 55 x 47 x 1¼ in (139.7 x 119.7 x 3.2 cm); acrylic and photography on panel
The French experimental artist Yves Klein (1928–62) set out to rid color of its emotional associations, freeing it to exist as a work of art in its own right. The *IKB* of the title stands for "International Klein Blue," an exceptionally intense blue that the artist patented as his own invention. In the late 1950s, Klein painted a series of pictures filled with this one vibrant blue. For his 1960 exhibition, naked women were smeared with this color and dragged across canvases on the floor.

AS IF TO CELEBRATE, I DISCOVERED A MOUNTAIN BLOOMING WITH RED FLOWERS
Anish Kapoor; 1981; wood, cement, polystyrene, pigment
This sculpture, by the Indian-born artist Anish Kapoor (b.1954), uses vivid red and yellow powdered pigments of the type associated with Hindu worship. "The act of putting pigment on these objects removes all traces of the hand," he explains. "They are not made, they are just there."

Loose, pure color gives the forms a ritualistic significance

Fresh approaches

IN THE POST-WAR PERIOD, artists began to divorce color from its traditional contexts. American painters, like Jackson Pollock (1912–56), started to apply colors in unusually direct and unconventional ways: paints – household emulsions, enamels, aluminum – were poured or splattered onto the canvas, with little intervention from traditional painting tools. For Pop artists (so called because they borrowed images from popular culture), Pollock's thick, "scribbled" paint still smacked of painterly brushwork. Andy Warhol (1928?–87) reacted by embracing new mechanical techniques, like silk-screen printing, and synthetic colors and mediums: his *Green Marilyn* uses fluorescent paints, overprinted with a photographic image, to suggest a machine-made object. While Warhol's paints were still mostly brushed by hand, Morris Louis (1912–62) dripped his thinned acrylic paints over raw, unprepared canvas. Color was finally freed from the distractions of surface texture and subject matter.

GREEN MARILYN
Andy Warhol; 1964; 20 x 16 in (50.8 x 40.6 cm);
silk screen on synthetic polymer paint on canvas
Warhol used gaudy color to make pop-culture images – here, a publicity photo of Marilyn Monroe – more provocative and artificially appealing. The silk-screen method was borrowed from the world of commercial fabric printing.

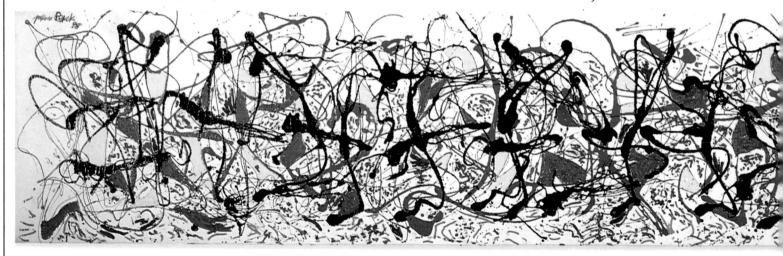

SUMMERTIME NO. 9A
Jackson Pollock; 1948; 33½ x 218½ in (84.8 x 555 cm); oil and enamel on canvas
Pollock's famous "drip and splash" style dates from 1947. It involved dribbling paint from a dried-out brush or a can onto a huge canvas – here, areas in the squiggles of black enamel paint have been filled in with primary colors. In this way, Pollock hoped to achieve a direct expression of his unconscious moods. The technique was inspired by Indian sand-painting, in which colored sands were trickled over one another. The texture of Pollock's pigments was all-important: he sometimes added sand or broken glass to create heavy impasto, working the paint with sticks, trowels, or knives.

Aluminum powder, used by Pollock in many works

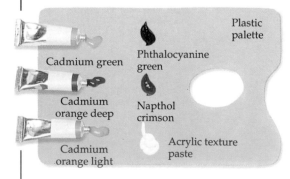

Plastic palette
Cadmium green
Phthalocyanine green
Cadmium orange deep
Napthol crimson
Cadmium orange light
Acrylic texture paste

THE ACRYLIC MEDIUM
Acrylic paint is pigment bound with a synthetic (plastic) resin. It dries quickly and can be mixed with more resin or water to create different types of surface finish. It is ideal for creating flat, hard-edged colors, but it can also be used in thin washes. Acrylic lines include many specially developed chemical colors, and texture paste for building impasto (left).

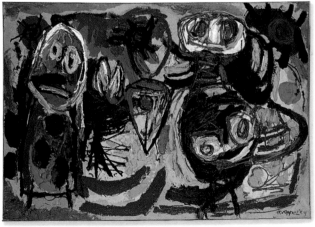

PEOPLE, BIRDS, AND SUN
Karel Appel; 1954; 68 x 95½ in (173 x 242.8 cm); oil on canvas
Many modern artists continued to use traditional techniques in an individual way. The Dutch artist Karel Appel (b.1921) applies his strong oil colors thickly and crudely to re-create the spontaneous imagery of his inner world. Paints, however, are always mixed, and never used straight from the tube.

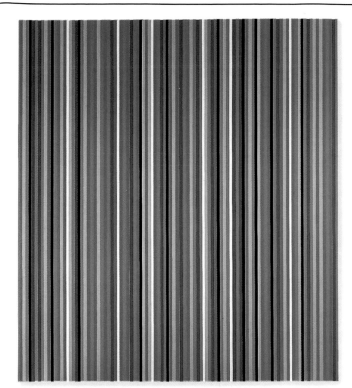

LUXOR

Bridget Riley; 1982; 88 x 77¾ in (223.5 x 197.5 cm); oil on linen

In her early color works, the British artist Bridget Riley (b.1931) exploited the flicker and vibration of curves and spirals. She soon decided, however, that "color energies need a virtually neutral vehicle if they are to develop uninhibited." Here, Riley has used plain vertical stripes in a limited palette inspired by Egyptian tomb paintings (below). The hues – echoing the desert, earth, water, sky, and greenery – interact with one another to generate their own space, colors, and light, while also retaining their individual intensity.

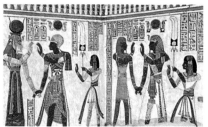

A photograph, owned by Riley, of a tomb painting from Luxor

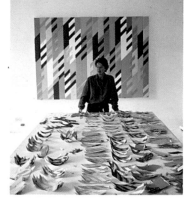

Riley analyzing color combinations

MIXING COLORS

Bridget Riley works in a meticulous way, carefully mixing her colors to achieve the exact hue and intensity desired. Color interaction is initially explored in small gouache color studies, moving on to full-size paper-and-gouache designs (as in the photograph above). The large-scale canvas is then marked up and painted entirely by hand – first in acrylics, then in oil.

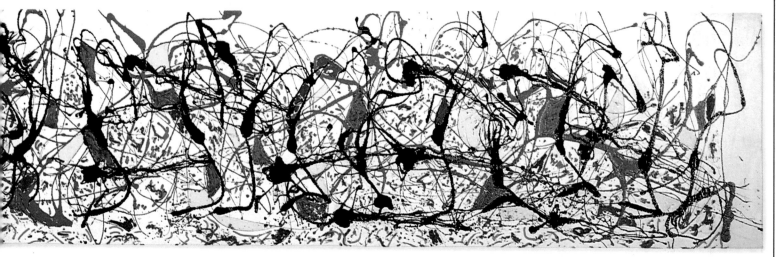

ALPHA-PHI

Morris Louis; 1961; 102 x 180¾ in (259.1 x 459.1 cm); acrylic on canvas

The American painter Morris Louis developed an innovative method that gave an independent life to color. He poured thinned Magna acrylic paint (one of the new lines) onto unprimed cotton canvas, so that the color soaked into the weave. In oil painting, the canvas must be primed (covered with a preparatory layer or ground) to prevent an oil, such as linseed, from destroying the fibers of the cloth. Acrylic allowed Louis to eliminate this barrier, so that the surface of the canvas seems to be stained with color. *Alpha-Phi* is just one of a series of paintings, entitled *Unfurleds*, in which this technique is used to breathtaking effect. The liquid color flows sensuously across the lower corners, bounding the vast empty space in between. The effect is one of pure liquid color, rather than of paint applied manually to a surface.

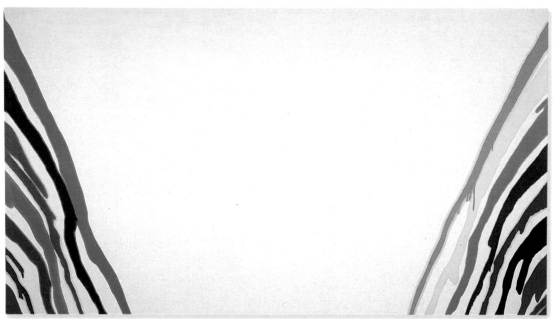

Glossary

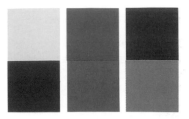

Complementary colors

"Additive" primaries The three primaries of colored light (orange-red, green, and blue-violet), from which all other colors can be mixed. These are different than the primaries of pigments, inks, and photographic emulsions ("subtractive" primaries).

"Additive" mixing The combining or "adding together" of the additive primaries, to create other colored lights.

Aerial perspective A coloristic effect, used in landscape backgrounds, in which colors are painted paler and bluer the farther they appear from the eye. This imitates colors in nature: blue light is scattered by the moist air of the intervening atmosphere.

Afterimage The image which remains after we stare fixedly at a color and then shift our gaze to a plain white or neutral surface. This "negative" image is the original color's "complementary" (below). This occurs because the eye tires quickly when it looks at one color intensely, and, for a moment, can only see the color that dominates the remainder of the spectrum.

Azurite A mineral pigment (copper carbonate): blue/blue-green.

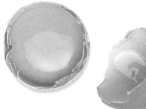

Egg, used in tempera painting

Brilliant colors Colors of high intensity and purity.

Broken color Mixed or tertiary color.

Cadmium colors Opaque pigments based on sulfides of the element cadmium.

Cangiante (Italian: "changing") A type of coloring that imitates shot silk, in which bright contrasting colors are alternated in highlight and shadow. Often used for the draperies of angels to create supernatural effects.

Chiaroscuro (Italian: "bright-dark") A type of coloring that uses extremes of light and shade to make illuminated forms appear three-dimensional. The contrasts are often used to give forms theatrical impact.

Chromium colors Opaque pigments based on compounds of the element chromium, such as viridian (a strong, cold green) and chrome yellow. Mainly used after the early 19th century.

Cobalt colors Pigments based on compounds of the element cobalt; the first cobalt pigment, cobalt blue, was discovered in 1802.

Complementary color The true contrast or "negative" color of any given hue: the color of the dominant wavelength that the hue absorbs is its complementary. When a color is mixed with its complementary (physically and optically – see "optical mixing"), both hues are neutralized (to a gray-black). When they are placed side by side, they intensify each other by contrast (see "afterimage" and "simultaneous contrast").

Cool colors Colors that tend toward blue, most obviously those in the blue-green-violet range. It has been shown that cool colors actually slow down the viewer's circulation, causing a slight drop in body temperature.

Copper resinate Transparent deep green glaze; verdigris (or other copper salt) in resin and oil.

Earth colors Natural pigments found in the ground, made up of iron oxides mixed with varying proportions of clay. The colors range from dull red, yellow, orange, and brown to black, and are found in the form of ochres, umbers, and siennas. Earth pigments can be burnt or roasted to produce warmer shades.

Gesso (Italian: "gypsum") A white plasterlike material, mixed with animal glue ("size"), for use as a preparatory layer ("ground") in early Italian panel painting.

Glaze Transparent paint.

Ground The preparatory surface for a painting.

Hue The apparent color of a visual sensation, described as "red," "blue," and so on.

Impasto Paint applied in thick, raised brushstrokes.

Lake pigment A soluble dye, which is formed into solid particles by being deposited on a powdered base such as chalk or aluminum oxide. Lakes are usually translucent when mixed with a medium, and are ideal for glazes.

Lead white An opaque white pigment, produced synthetically.

Local color Color as it appears in nature (such as green for grass).

Luminosity Giving the appearance of conveying a large amount of light.

Medium A binding agent, like oil or egg, which makes the particles of pigment stick together and also binds them to the prepared surface.

Modeling The building up of forms in lights and darks (to suggest light and shaded areas), to make them look three-dimensional.

Neutral colors "Colors" on the white-gray-black scale.

Opaque Unable to transmit light: not transparent. An opaque pigment has good hiding power (obscuring the ground or color beneath it).

Optical mixing When colors are blended in the eye, rather than being physically mixed together.

Organic pigments Pigments of animal or plant origin (often unstable).

Palette Both the surface on which the painter lays out his colors, and the range of colors chosen.

Pigment The coloring matter (usually in the form of a powder) used in painting.

Primary colors The fundamental colors, which cannot be created by mixture, but which can be combined to create other colors. The purest primary colors of pigment are magenta (bluish red), cyan (greenish blue), and yellow (used in modern color printing), which are more simply perceived as red, blue, and yellow.

Priming Preparing a surface (ground) for painting on.

Resin A sticky natural substance from plants or trees, used to make glazes and varnishes, or as a binding medium.

Saturation The depth or "colorfulness" of a color, and its freedom from gray.

Secondary color A color made by mixing two primaries together.

Sfumato (Italian: "smoky") A type of coloring that uses midrange colors, in which the transitions between colors are softened and blurred to give a naturalistic misty appearance.

Shot colour *Cangiante* coloring (above) that imitates the different colored threads in woven silk; these change from one hue to the next according to the angle of the light.

Simultaneous contrast The effect produced when contrasting or complementary colors are placed next to one another: the colors will appear heightened in intensity, and totally dissimilar to one another.

Spectral colors The constituent colors of white light.

Stable pigments Pigments which do not fade, or alter chemically, over time.

Shot color

"Subtractive" mixing The blending of pigments, in which colors absorb or "subtract" light. The resultant color is provided by the dominant wavelength that is not absorbed by the pigment. When the three subtractive primaries are mixed, they produce gray-black.

"Subtractive" primaries The pure primaries used in modern color printing: magenta, cyan, and yellow.

Terra verde (Italian: "green earth") A natural, dull green pigment, made from clay, containing the mineral glauconite or celadonite.

Tertiary color A color produced by mixing two secondaries.

Tone The degree of lightness or darkness of a color.

Ultramarine An exceptionally pure blue pigment extracted from the lapis lazuli stone. Synthetic equivalent produced since c.1830.

Undermodeling The preliminary depiction of forms, in broad terms of light and shade, during the early stages of a painting.

Verdigris A copper-based green pigment, often mixed with resin to make the deep green glaze copper resinate.

Vermilion An opaque red pigment, made from the mineral cinnabar, and produced artificially (mercuric sulfide) from ancient times.

Warm colors Colors that tend toward yellow, most obviously those in the red-orange-yellow range. Warm colors stimulate the viewer's circulation and cause a slight rise in body temperature.

Wavelength The distance between two adjacent identical points on a light wave, which gives a spectral light its apparent color quality.

Itten's color star

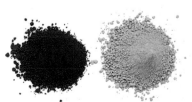

Red ochre   Yellow ochre

Featured works

Look here to find the location of, and complete details about, the works featured in the book.

This section also includes photographic acknowledgments, although further information can be found under "Acknowledgments" (p. 64).

Every effort has been made to trace the copyright holders and we apologize in advance for any unintentional omissions. We would be pleased to insert the appropriate acknowledgment in any subsequent edition of this publication.

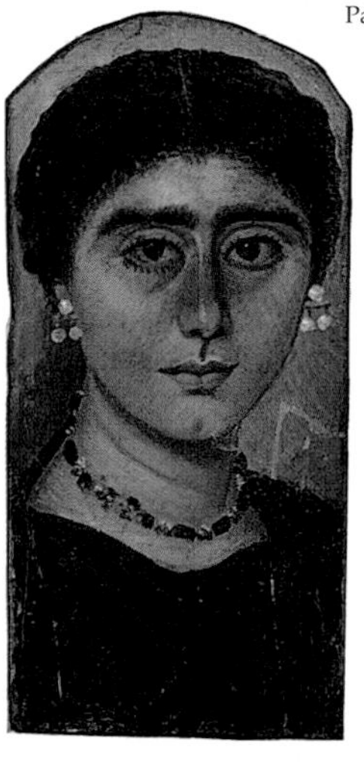

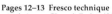

Romano-Egyptian Funerary Portrait (p. 9)

Key: *t*: top; *b*: bottom; *c*: center; *l*: left; *r*: right

Abbreviations:
AIC: The Art Institute of Chicago, All Rights Reserved; **BAL:** Bridgeman Art Library; **BIF:** Bibliothèque de l'Institut de France, Paris; **BL:** By Permission of the British Library; **BM:** The Trustees of the British Museum, London; **BN:** Bibliothèque Nationale, Paris; **FC:** © Frick Collection, New York; **FW:** Fitzwilliam Museum, Cambridge, UK; **HA:** © Hunterian Art Gallery, University of Glasgow; **ML:** Musée du Louvre, Paris; **MO:** Musée d'Orsay, Paris; **NGL:** Reproduced by Courtesy of the Trustees of the National Gallery, London; **NGW:** © National Gallery of Art, Washington; **PC:** Private Collection; **SC:** Scala; **TG:** Tate Gallery, London; **V&A:** Courtesy of the Board of Trustees of the Victoria and Albert Museum, London

Front cover: clockwise from top left: Runge's color sphere (p36); Harris's prismatic color wheel (p36); Rose and green gandoura (p57); first plate of Goethe's "Theory of Colors" (p36); *The Night Café* (p46); gilding materials (p11); *The Wish of the Young St. Francis to Become a Soldier* (p15); *The Great One* (p9) **Inside front flap:** *b*: *The Coronation of the Virgin* (p14). **Back cover:** clockwise from top left: Florentine scales (p14); *The Toreador Fresco* (p12); *Light and Color (Goethe's Theory)* (p37); Turner's paint box (p37); *Ginevra de' Benci* (p20); Chalice of the Abbot Suger of St. Denis (p10); *The Court of Justinian* (detail, p10); *Maestà* (pp10–11); Goethe's color triangle (p36); *The Adoration of the Magi* (p17); florins (p14); center: *Fatata te Miti (By the Sea)* (p43)

p1 (Half Title): *The Adoration of the Magi* (p17); **p2:** *tl*: Stained glass windows in the Church of St. Peter and St. Paul (p43); *tc*: Rose and green gandoura (p57) *c*: *The Great One* (p9); *cr*: Persian illuminated manuscript, BM (p27); *bl*: Restored *Libyan Sibyl* (p28); *br*: *As if to Celebrate, I Discovered a Mountain Blooming with Red Flowers* (p59) **p3 (Title Page):** *tl*: Frontispiece of "Colors and Applications"(p44); *tr, cr*: Details of first plate of Goethe's "Theory of Colors" (p36); *c, bl*: *The Wish of the Young St. Francis to Become a Soldier* (p15) **p4:** *tl*: Atsuita Karaori kimono (p49); *cl*: *The Ascension of Mohammed* (p4); *cr*: Persian tiling (p55); *bc*: Theban brushes(p8); *br*: *Portrait of Félix Fénéon in 1890*, Paul Signac (p45)

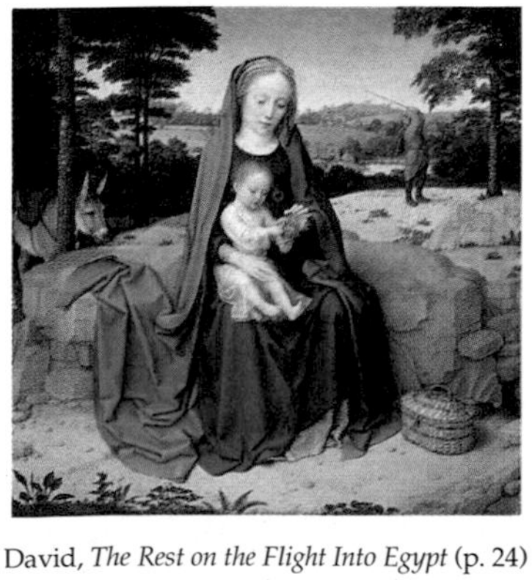

David, *The Rest on the Flight Into Egypt* (p. 24)

Pages 6–7 What is color?
p6: *c, b* (detail): *Study for a Portrait of Bonnard*, Edouard Vuillard, Musée du Petit Palais, Paris/Photothèque des Musées de la Ville de Paris/© DACS 1993 **p7:** *tc*: Printers' inks; *tr*: *Political Drama*, Robert Delaunay, NGW, Gift of Joseph H. Hazen Foundation, Inc/© ADAGP, Paris, and DACS, London 1993; *bl, c*: *Horse* (Red side and blue side), Alexander Calder, NGW, Gift of Mrs. Paul Mellon in Honor of the 50th Anniversary of the NGW/© ADAGP, Paris, and DACS, London 1993; *br*: *Runge's Color Sphere Depicted as a Star*, Johannes Itten/© DACS 1993

Pages 8–9 Ancient materials
p8: *tl*: *Rotunda frieze*, Lascaux Caves, Caisse Nationale des Monuments Historiques et des Sites/© DACS 1993; *cr*: *Food for a Banquet*, Ardea, London; *bc*: Egyptian palette, BM **p9:** *t*: *Woman Being Flagellated and Dancing Bacchus*, Villa dei Misteri, Pompeii/SC; *bl*: Theban brushes, BM; *bcl*: *The Great One*, BM/Photo © Michael Holford; *br*: *Romano-Egyptian Funerary Portrait*, ML

Pages 10–11 The splendor of gold
p10: *tl*: Chalice of the Abbot Suger of St. Denis, © 1992 NGW, Widener Collection; *cl, tr* (detail): *The Court of Justinian*, San Vitale, Ravenna/SC; *bl*: *The Ascension of Mohammed* (from a Persian illuminated manuscript), BL **pp10–11** *b, tl*: *Maestà* (front), Duccio, Museo dell'Opera Metropolitana/SC **p11:** *tc*: Sicilian textile, V&A; *cr*: gilding materials

Pages 12–13 Fresco technique
p12: *l*: Arena Chapel, Padua/SC; *tr*: *The Toreador Fresco*, National Archaeological Museum, Athens/BAL; *cr, br* (detail): *Lamentation over the Dead Christ*, Giotto, Arena Chapel, Padua/SC **p13:** *c, br* (detail): *The Tribute Money*, Masaccio, Brancacci Chapel, Chiesa del Carmine, Florence/SC; *bl*: The King's Room, Würzburg Rezidenz, Würzburg/SC

Pages 14–15 The value of color
p14: *tl* (detail): Early 12th-century treatise, Trinity College, Cambridge/BAL; *tr*: 17th-century Florentine scales, Science Museum, Florence/Photo: Franca Principe; *cr*: Florentine florins, BM; *b*: *The Coronation of the Virgin*, Enguerrand Quarton, Musée Pierre de Luxembourg, Villeneuve-Les-Avignon/Photo: Daspet **p15:** *c, cl* (detail): *The Kiss of Judas*, Giotto, Arena Chapel, Padua/SC; *t, cr* (detail): *The Wish of the Young St. Francis to Become a Soldier*, Sassetta, NGL; *br, bc* (detail): *The Crucifixion*, Masaccio, Museo di Capodimonte, Naples/SC

Pages 16–17 Egg tempera painting
p16: *tl*: Page of Cennino Cennini's "*Il Libro dell'Arte*," Biblioteca Medicea Laurenziana, Florence/Photo: Donato Pineider; *tr*: Back of panel, *Saint Paul*, Bernardo Daddi © 1993 NGW, Andrew W. Mellon Collection *b*: Three parts of an altarpiece: (*l*: *Adoring Saints*; *r*: *Adoring Saints*; *c*: *The Coronation of the Virgin*), Lorenzo Monaco, NGL **p17:** *tl*: *The Adoration of the Magi*, Fra Angelico and Filippo Lippi © 1993 NGW, Samuel H. Kress Collection; *tr*: "The Story of Thamyris", from Boccaccio's "De Claris Mulieribus," BN/BAL; *cl*: (detail) *Maestà* (front), Duccio, Museo dell'Opera Metropolitana/SC; *bl*: Paint cross-section (flesh of hand) from *David*, Santa Croce Altarpiece, Ugolino di Nerio, NGL; *br*: *Virgin and Child with St. Andrew and St. Peter*, Cima da Conegliano, National Gallery of Scotland, Edinburgh

Pages 18–19 Color, light, and narrative
p18: *c, tl* (detail): *The Resurrected Christ*, Isenheim altarpiece, Grünewald, Musée d'Unterlinden, Colmar, France/Photo: O. Zimmermann; *cl*: *The Small Crucifixion*, Grünewald, © 1993 NGW, Samuel H. Kress Collection; *bl*: Engraving after a miniature from a 14th-century edition of St. Bridget of Sweden's "Revelations", Mary Evans Picture Library, London; *br*: *The Annunciation*, Piero della Francesca, San Francisco, Arezzo/SC **p19:** *l, br*: *Adoration of the Shepherds*, El Greco, Prado, Madrid/SC; *tr*: *The Alba Madonna*, Raphael, NGW, Andrew W. Mellon Collection

Pages 20–21 Leonardo's naturalism
p20: *tr, c*: Leonardo Manuscripts, The Royal Collection © 1993 H.M. Queen Elizabeth II; *br, bl* (detail): *Ginevra de' Benci*, Leonardo da Vinci, NGW, Ailsa Mellon Bruce Fund **p21:** *t*: *The Virgin, Infant Jesus, and St. Anne*, Leonardo da Vinci, ML/RMN; *bl*: Leonardo Manuscript, BIF

Pages 22–23 Coloring in oils
p22: *cl*: Illustration of madder plant, Winsor and Newton, Harrow, Middlesex; *r, bl* (paint analyses): *The Annunciation*, Jan van Eyck, NGW, Andrew W. Mellon Collection; **p23:** *tl*: *Tarquin and Lucretia*, Titian, FW; *tr* (paint analyses), *c* (X-ray): Hamilton Kerr Institute/FW; *br, bl* (detail), *Minerva Protects Pax from Mars (Peace and War)*, Rubens, NGL

Pages 24–25 Color and space
p24: *tr*: *Paesaggio*, National Museum, Naples/SC; *cr, cl* (detail): *The Rest on the Flight Into Egypt*, Gerard David, NGW, Andrew W. Mellon Collection; *bl, br*: *Landscape with Hagar and the Angel*, Claude Lorrain, NGL **p25:** *t*: *The Dogana and Santa Maria della Salute, Venice*, J.M.W. Turner, NGW, Given in memory of Governor Alvan T. Fuller by the Fuller Foundation, Inc.; *b, c* (detail): *Wivenhoe Park, Essex*, John Constable, NGW, Widener Collection

Pages 26–27 The Venetian School
p26 *tl*: Bird's-eye view of Venice, Jacopo de'Barbari, BM; *tr*: *Christ in Judgment and the Four Evangelists*, Pala d'Oro, San Marco, Venice/SC; *br, bl* (detail): *Danäe*, Titian, Museo del Prado, Madrid/SC **p27:** *t*: *The Family of Darius before Alexander*, Veronese, NGL; *cl*: Persian illuminated manuscript, BM; *c* (detail): *Tarquin and Lucretia*, Titian, FW; *br*: Medieval dyers, Color Museum, Bradford, UK

Pages 28–29 The restoration of color
p28: *tr* (detail): Eve's face, *Garden of Eden* (central ceiling panel; before restoration), Sistine Ceiling, Michelangelo, SC; *l*: *The Libyan Sybil* (after restoration), Sistine Ceiling, Michelangelo © Nippon Television Network Corporation 1993; *c*: *The Libyan Sybil* (before restoration), Sistine Ceiling, Michelangelo, SC; *br*: *The Feast of the Gods* (before restoration), Giovanni Bellini and Titian, NGW, Widener Collection **p29:** *t, br* (paint analyses): *The Feast of the Gods*, NGW, Widener Collection; *bc*: Florentine 16th-century Small Ewer, NGW, Widener Collection

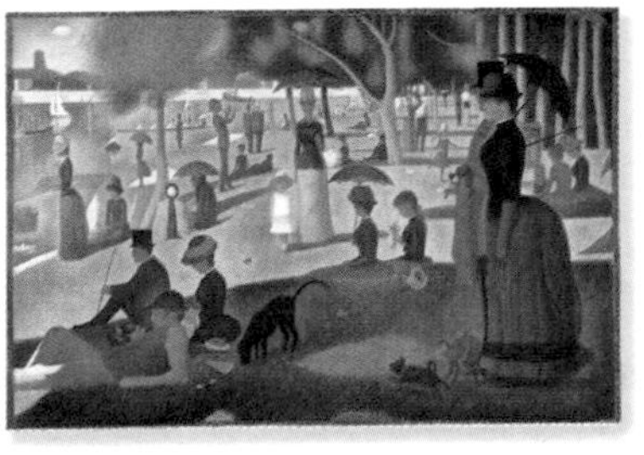

Seurat, *A Sunday Afternoon on the Island of La Grande Jatte* (p. 44)

Pages 30–31 Chiaroscuro: light and shadow
p30: *tl*: Candle, Science Photo Library; *l, bl* (detail): *The Calling of St. Matthew*, Caravaggio, San Luigi dei Francesi, Rome/SC; *r, br* (detail): *The Repentant Magdalene*, Georges de La Tour, NGW, Ailsa Mellon Bruce Fund **p31:** *tl*: *A Woman Bathing in a Stream*, Rembrandt, NGL; *cr*: *Rembrandt's Studio with a Model*, Rembrandt, Ashmolean Museum, Oxford; *br*: *Still Life with Melon and Peaches*, Edouard Manet, NGW, Gift of Eugene and Agnes E. Meyer

Pages 32–33 Painting with light
p32: *l, br* (detail): *The Girl with the Red Hat*, Jan Vermeer, NGW, Andrew W. Mellon Collection; *tr*: Room-type camera obscura, from Athanasius Kircher's "*Ars Magna Lucis et Umbrae*," Rome, 1649 **p33:** *t*: *A Lady Taking Tea*, Jean-Baptiste Chardin, HA; *bl, br* (detail): *Still Life*, Henri Fantin-Latour, NGW, Chester Dale Collection

Pages 34–35 Rococo decoration
p34: *l*: *Hollyhocks*, Jean-Honoré Fragonard, FC; *tr*: *Love As Conqueror*, Jean-Honoré Fragonard, NGW, In Memory of Kate Seney Simpson; *c*: View of the Boucher Room, FC; *bc*: Chinese jar and Sèvres vase, FC **p35:** *tl*: *A Young Girl Reading*, Jean-Honoré Fragonard, NGW, Gift of Mrs. Mellon Bruce in Memory of her Father, Andrew W. Mellon; *r*: *Hollyhocks*, Jean-Honoré Fragonard, FC; *c*: Gobelins tapestry, ML/RMN; *bl*: Gilt bronze tripod table, FC; *br*: "A Tintbook of Historical Colors Suitable for Decorative Work," John Oliver, London

Pages 36–37 Goethe's color theory
p36: *tl*: First plate of Goethe's "Theory of Colors"; *l*: *Morning*, Philipp Otto Runge, Kunsthalle, Hamburg/Artothek; *cr*: Color sphere, Philipp Otto Runge, Kunsthalle, Hamburg; *br*: Moses Harris's prismatic color wheel, from "The Natural System of Colors," Royal Academy of Arts Library, London **p37:** *tl*: Diagram of Goethe and Newton's color spectrums from Goethe's "Theory of Colors"; *cl*: Goethe's color wheel from his "Theory of Colors"; *tr*: Title page of Charles Eastlake's translation of Goethe's "Theory of Colors," BL; *bl*: *Shade and Darkness, the Evening of the Deluge*, J.M.W. Turner, TG; *cr*: *Light and Color (Goethe's Theory) – Morning after the Deluge – Moses Writing the Book of Genesis*, J.M.W. Turner, TG; *br*: Turner's paint box, TG

Pages 38–39 Harmony and contrast
p38: *tr*: Delacroix's palette, V&A; *cl*: Delacroix's color triangle, Musée Condé, Chantilly; *br, bl* (detail): *The Expulsion of Heliodorus from the Temple*, Eugène Delacroix, Saint-Sulpice, Paris/Lauros-Giraudon **p39:** *tl*: Chevreul's color wheel, BN; *tc*: Photo of Chevreul, BN; *c, b* (detail): *Our English Coasts, (Strayed Sheep)*, William Holman Hunt, TG; *r*: Perkin's original mauveine, Color Museum, Bradford, UK

Pages 40–41 Impressions of nature
p40: *l*: Renoir's list of colors, Document Archives Durand-Ruel, Paris; *br, bl* (paint analyses): *Boating on the Seine*, Auguste Renoir, NGL **p41:** *t, r* (detail): *Woman with a Parasol – Madame Monet and Her Son*, Claude Monet, NGW, Collection of Mr. and Mrs. Paul Mellon; *br*: Monet's palette, Musée Marmottan, Paris

Pages 42–43 Poetic color
p42: *l, c*: Whistler's palette, paints, and brushes, HA, Birnie Philip Bequest; *r*: *The White Girl (Symphony in White, No. 1)*, James Abbott McNeill Whistler, NGW, Harris Whittemore Collection; **p43:** *tl, tc* (detail): Stained glass windows, south aisle of the Church of St. Peter and St. Paul, Cattistock, Reproduced by Courtesy of the Friends of Cattistock Church, Dorset; *tr*: *Laus Veneris*, Edward Coley Burne-Jones, Laing Art Gallery, Newcastle upon Tyne (Tyne and Wear Museums); *c*: *Holy Women at the Tomb*, Maurice Denis, Musée du Prieuré, Saint-German-en-Laye/Lauros-Giraudon, Paris/© DACS 1993; *bl*: *Fatata te Miti (By the Sea)*, Paul Gauguin, NGW, Chester Dale Collection; *r*: Gauguin's palette, MO/RMN

Pages 44–45 Color science
p44: *tl*: Microphotograph from *A Sunday Afternoon on the Island of La Grande Jatte*, Georges Seurat, © AIC/Photo: I. Fielder; *r*: *Study for "Les Poseuses,"* Georges Seurat, MO, Paris; *bl*: Frontispiece of Rood's "Colors and Applications," BIF; *br*: *A Sunday Afternoon on the Island of La Grande Jatte*, Georges Seurat, © AIC, Helen Bartlett Memorial Collection **p45:** *t, c* (detail): *Against the Enamel of a Background Rhythmic with Beats and Angles, Tones and Colors, Portrait of Félix Fénéon in 1890*, Paul Signac, PC, New York/Photo: Malcolm Varon, NYC/© DACS 1993; *br*: Charles Henry's Aesthetic Protractor from "*Rapporteur Esthétique*," PC

Pages 46–47 A means of expression
p46: *b*: *The Night Café*, Vincent van Gogh, Yale University Art Gallery, Bequest of Stephen Carlton Clark BA, 1903 **p46:** *l*: *The Scream*, Edvard Munch, © Munch Museum, Munch Estate, Bono, Oslo/DACS, London 1993; *tr*: *Two Women on the Shore*, Edvard Munch, NGW, Gift of the Sarah G. Epstein and Lionel C. Epstein Family Collection, in Honor of the 50th Anniversary of the NGW; *cr*: *Two Women on the Shore*, Edvard Munch, NGW, Print Purchase Fund (Rosenwald Collection) and Ailsa Mellon Bruce Fund© Munch Museum, Munch Estate, Bono, Oslo/DACS, London 1993; *b*: *Dresden Houses*,

Continued on p. 64

Index

Ernst Ludwig Kirchner, NGW, Ruth and Jacob Kainen Collection, Gift (Partial and Promised) in Honor of the 50th Anniversary of the NGW

Pages 48–49 Patterns of the East
p48: *c: Sketch for the Balcony,* James Abbott McNeill Whistler, HA, Birnie Philip Bequest; *l: View over the Bay of Shinagawa, The Fourth Month,* from the series "The 12 Months of Mimami", Kiyonaga, BM; *br: Catching Fireflies,* Choki, BM **p49:** *l: Fulfillment,* Gustav Klimt, Musée de Strasbourg; *tr: Atsuita Karaori kimono,* Collection of Tokyo National Museum; *c:* Japanese folding screen, Collection les Indiennes, Paris; *bl: Le Père Tanguy,* Vincent van Gogh, PC, Paris/BAL; *br: Promenade des Nourrices, Frise des Fiacres (Street Scene),* Pierre Bonnard, MO, Paris/RMN/© ADAGP /SPADEM, Paris, and DACS, London 1993

Pages 50–51 Picasso's changing palette
p50: *tr:* Photo of Picasso in his studio, Photo: Michel Sima/Selon; *l: Madame Camus,* Edgar Degas, NGW, Chester Dale Collection; *br: The Tragedy,* Pablo Picasso, NGW, Chester Dale Collection/© DACS 1993 **p51:** *l: Nude Woman,* Pablo Picasso, NGW, Ailsa Mellon Bruce Fund/© DACS 1993; *tr: Houses in Provence,* Paul Cézanne, NGW, Collection of Mr. and Mrs. Paul Mellon; *c: Las Meninas,* Diego Velázquez, Museo del Prado, Madrid; *br: Las Meninas: Infanta Margerita Maria No. 27,* Pablo Picasso, Museu Pablo Picasso, Barcelona/© DACS 1993

Pages 52–53 Color and music
p52: *tr:* Newton's color wheel; *bl:* Frontispiece and page from *"De Colori,"* by Matteo Zaccolini, Biblioteca Medicea Laurenziana, Florence; *br: Mary, Queen of Heaven,* Master of the Saint Lucy Legend, NGW, Samuel H. Kress Collection **p53:** *t: Junger Wald (Young Forest),* Paul Klee, NGW, Gift (Partial and Promised) of Lili-Charlotte Sarnoff in Honor of the 50th Anniversary of the NGW/© DACS 1993 *cl: Improvisation 31 (Sea Battle),* Wassily Kandinsky, NGW, Ailsa Mellon Bruce Fund/© ADAGP, Paris and DACS, London 1993; *c:* Color Sonatina in Red, Ludwig Hirschfeld-Mack, Bauhaus Archiv, Museum für Gestaltung, Berlin; Photo of Arnold Schönberg, Photographie Musée Nationale d'Art Moderne, Centre Georges Pompidou, Paris/© SPADEM, Paris, and DACS, London

1993; *br: The Song of the Vowels,* Joan Miró, Museum of Modern Art, New York, Mrs. Simon Guggenheim Fund, special contribution in Honor of Dorothy C. Miller, © ADAGP, Paris, and DACS, London 1993

Pages 54–55 Oriental light
p54: *tr:* Kairouan, the Grand Mosque, World Pictures; *cl:* Moucharabieh in blue and green, Musée Matisse, Nice; *c:* Photo of Klee and Macke, 1914, Bildarchiv Felix Klee, Bern, Photo: Louis Moilliet; *b: Kairouan I,* Auguste Macke, Staatsgalerie für Moderne Kunst, Munich/© Artothek **p55:** *t: Persische Nachtigallen (Persian Nightingales),* Paul Klee, NGW, Gift (Partial and Promised) in Honor of the 50th Anniversary of the NGW, PC, New York/© DACS 1993; *b:* Paint box, Winsor and Newton, Harrow, Middlesex; *br:* Persian tiling, Robert Harding Associates, London

Pages 56–57 Matisse's pure color
p56: *tr: Henri Matisse,* André Derain, TG/© ADAGP, Paris, and DACS, London 1993; *l:* Baule face mask, Ivory Coast, Werner Forman Archive; *cl:* Reliquary Obi mask, Gabon, Werner Forman Archive; *br: Harmony in Red,* Henri Matisse, Hermitage, Leningrad/Artothek/© Succession H. Matisse/DACS 1993 **p57:** *tl:* Photo of Henri Matisse, © Hélène Adant/Rapho; *l:* Moroccan bonnet from the Collection H. Matisse, Musée Matisse, Nice; *c:* Rose and green gandoura, Morocco, Musée Matisse, Nice; *r: Beasts of the Sea,* Henri Matisse, NGW, Ailsa Mellon Bruce Fund © Succession H. Matisse/DACS 1993

Pages 58–59 Abstract power
p58: *tr: Wall Hanging in Red and Green,* Gunta Stölz, Bauhaus Archiv, Museum für Gestaltung, Berlin, Photo: Hermann Kiessling/© DACS 1993; *l: Diamond Painting in Red, Yellow, and Blue,* Piet Mondrian, NGW, Gift of Herbert and Nannette Rothschild/© DACS 1993; *br:* First plate of "The Interaction of Color," Joseph Albers, Bauhaus Archiv, Museum für Gestaltung, Berlin, Photo: Markus Hawlik/© DACS 1993 **p59:** *t, l* (detail): *Red, Black, White on Yellow,* Mark Rothko, NGW, Gift of Mrs. Paul Mellon, in Honour of the 50th Anniversary of the NGW/© 1993 Kate Rothko-Prizel and Christopher Rothko/ARS New York; *bl: IKB 79,*

Yves Klein, TG/© ADAGP, Paris, and DACS, London 1993; *br: As if to Celebrate, I Discovered a Mountain Blooming with Red Flowers,* Anish Kapoor, TG

Pages 60–61 Fresh approaches
p60: *tl: Green Marilyn,* Andy Warhol, NGW, Gift of William C. Seitz and Irma S. Seitz in Honor of the 50th Anniversary of the NGW/© 1993 The Andy Warhol Foundation for the Visual Arts, Inc.; *br: People, Birds, and Sun,* Karel Appel, TG/De Tuip Pers, Holland **pp60–61** *Summertime No. 9A,* Jackson Pollock, TG/© 1993 Pollock Krasner Foundation/ARS, New York **p61:** *tl: Luxor,* © Bridget Riley, 1993 Glasgow Museums: Art Gallery and Museum, Kelvingrove; *tr:* Photo of Bridget Riley, © Bridget Riley; *tc:* Tomb painting, Photo © Bridget Riley; *br: Alpha-Phi,* Morris Louis, TG

Pages 62–63 Glossary; Featured works
p62: *tl: Itten's color star (p7); cr* (detail): *The Feast of the Gods (p29); p63: tl: Romano-Egyptian Funerary Portrait (p9); bl: The Rest on the Flight Into Egypt (p24); cr: A Sunday Afternoon on the Island of La Grande Jatte (p44)*

Acknowledgments

Key: *t:* top; *b:* bottom; *c:* center; *l:* left; *r:* right

Photography for Dorling Kindersley:
Philip Gatward: **p6:** *tr* Philippe Sebert: **p9:** *tr*
p44: *tr* Susanna Price: **p8:** *bl*; **p9:** *cl, bcr*; **p13:** *t, tr*; **p14:** *cl*; **p16:** *cl*; **p17:** *c*; **p41:** *br* Edward Woodman: **p11:** *cr* Andy Crawford: **p20:** *cl*; **p50:** *tc* Alison Harris: **p21:** *br*; **p44:** *bl* Dave King: **p52:** *tl*

Artworks:
Simon Murrell: **p45:** *bc* Tony Graham: **p6:** *cl*; **p13:** *tc*; **p46:** *c* Claire Pegrum: **p46:** *tr*; **p48:** *tl*

Loan of materials:
A.P. Fitzpatrick Art Materials, Studio 1, 10–22 Barnabas Road, London E9 5SB: **p8:** *bl*; **p9:** *cl, bcr*; **p13:** *tl, tr*; **p14:** *cl*; **p17:** *c*; **p22:** *c*; **p27:** *bl, bc, cr*; **p31:** *bl* L. Cornelissen & Son Ltd., 105 Great Russell Street, London WC1B 3RY: **p8:** *br*; **p22:** *tl*; **p25:** *cl* Tony Street, Covent Garden Market: **p8:** *bl*; **p17:** *c* Camden Passage Antiques, London **p50:** *tcr* G.D. Warder and Sons, Gilders **p11:** *cr*

Dorling Kindersley would like to thank:
The staff at the National Gallery of Art, Washington, DC: especially Francis Smyth and Samantha Williams in the Editor's Office for their unstinting help and attention to detail; Barbara Berrie and Melanie Gifford in the Conservation Department for their meticulous technical advice; and all the other curators and conservators who helped on this project. Special thanks also to: Dr. Ashok Roy, Scientific Adviser to the National Gallery, London, for his expert technical advice, particularly with regard to pigments; Inge Fiedler at the Art Institute of Chicago; Philip Steadman for advice on camera obscuras; Bridget Riley for the loan of photographs; Inder Jamwal at John Oliver Ltd., London; Alan Fitzpatrick and Pip Seymour at A.P. Fitzpatrick Art Materials for their interest and enthusiasm, as well as the loan of a wide range of materials; the staff at Cornelissen's. Thanks are also due to Peter Jones for his research and editorial contributions; Job Rabkin for additional picture research; Susannah Steel; the Dorling Kindersley studio for additional photography; and Hilary Bird for the index.

Author's acknowledgments:
I would like to thank the following people for their kind help with this book: Francis Smyth, at the National Gallery of Art, Washington, DC, for her hospitality and advice; Barbara Berrie and Melanie Gifford, in the Conservation Department, and Ashok Roy and Marika Spring, in the Scientific and Conservation Departments of the National Gallery, London, for their unstinting attention to detail and generous technical comments; and Ian Chilvers for the loan of invaluable reference material.

Additional thanks are due to Keith, Jay, and Louis Shadwick for their patience and support, and to the following members of the Eyewitness Art team: Claire Pegrum (for her innovative designs), Gwen Edmonds (for overseeing the project), Julia Harris-Voss, Jo Evans, Job Rabkin (for their painstaking research). With a special thank you to my editor, Luisa Caruso, for her thoroughness and perfectionism.